D1606068

RILKE AND JUGENDSTIL

UNIVERSITY OF NORTH CAROLINA
STUDIES IN THE GERMANIC LANGUAGES
AND LITERATURES

Initiated by RICHARD JENTE (1949–1952), established by F. E. COENEN (1952–1968)

SIEGFRIED MEWS, EDITOR
Publication Committee: Department of Germanic Languages

79. Siegfried Mews and Herbert Knust, eds. ESSAYS ON BRECHT: THEATER AND POLITICS. 1974. Pp. xiv, 241. Cloth $11.95.
80. Donald G. Daviau and George J. Buelow. THE *ARIADNE AUF NAXOS* OF HUGO VON HOFMANNSTHAL AND RICHARD STRAUSS. 1975. Pp. x, 274. Cloth $12.75.
81. Elaine E. Boney. RAINER MARIA RILKE: *DUINESIAN ELEGIES*. German Text with English Translation and Commentary. 2nd ed. 1977.Pp. xii, 153. Cloth $10.75.
82. Jane K. Brown. GOETHE'S CYCLICAL NARRATIVES: *DIE UNTER-HALTUNGEN DEUTSCHER AUSGEWANDERTEN* AND *WILHELM MEISTERS WANDERJAHRE*. 1975. Pp. x, 144. Cloth $10.25.
83. Flora Kimmich. SONNETS OF CATHARINA VON GREIFFEN-BERG: METHODS OF COMPOSITION. 1975. Pp. x, 132. Cloth $11.50.
84. Herbert W. Reichert. FRIEDRICH NIETZSCHE'S IMPACT ON MODERN GERMAN LITERATURE. FIVE ESSAYS. 1975. Pp. xxii, 129. Cloth $9.00.
85. James C. O'Flaherty, Timothy F. Sellner, Robert M. Helm, eds. STUDIES IN NIETZSCHE AND THE CLASSICAL TRADITION. 1976. Pp. xviii, 278. Cloth $14.95.
86. Alan P. Cottrell. GOETHE'S *FAUST*. SEVEN ESSAYS. 1976. Pp. xvi, 143. Cloth $11.50.
87. Hugo Bekker. FRIEDRICH VON HAUSEN. INQUIRIES INTO HIS POETRY. Pp. x, 159. 1977. Cloth $12.95.
88. H. G. Huettich. THEATER IN THE PLANNED SOCIETY: CONTEMPORARY DRAMA IN THE GERMAN DEMOCRATIC REPUBLIC IN ITS HISTORICAL, POLITICAL, AND CULTURAL CONTEXT. Pp. xvi, 174. 1978. Cloth $11.50.
89. Donald G. Daviau, ed. THE LETTERS OF ARTHUR SCHNITZLER TO HERMANN BAHR. Pp. xii, 183. 1978. Cloth $13.95.
90. Karl Eugene Webb. RAINER MARIA RILKE AND *JUGENDSTIL*: AFFINITIES, INFLUENCES, ADAPTATIONS. Pp. x, 137. 1978. Cloth $12.95.

For other volumes in the "Studies" see pages 136–37.

Send orders to: (U.S. and Canada)
The University of North Carolina Press, P.O. Box 2288
Chapel Hill, N.C. 27514
(All other countries) Feffer and Simons, Inc., 31 Union Square, New York, N.Y. 10003

NUMBER NINETY

UNIVERSITY
OF NORTH CAROLINA
STUDIES IN
THE GERMANIC LANGUAGES
AND LITERATURES

1. Jan Toorop: "Maiden with Swans" (Rijksmuseum, Amsterdam)

Rainer Maria Rilke
and
Jugendstil

Affinities, Influences, Adaptations

by
Karl Eugene Webb

CHAPEL HILL
THE UNIVERSITY OF NORTH CAROLINA PRESS
1978

Library of Congress Cataloging in Publication Data

Webb, Karl Eugene, 1938–
  Rainer Maria Rilke and Jugendstil.

  (Studies in the Germanic languages and literatures;
no. 90 ISSN 0081-8593)
  Bibliography: pp. 127–31.
  Includes index.
  1. Rilke, Rainer Maria, 1875–1926—Criticism and
interpretation. 2. Art nouveau. I. Title.
II. Series: Studies in the Germanic languages and
literatures (Chapel Hill, N.C.); no. 90.

PT2635.I65Z959   831'.9'12   77-10430
ISBN 0-8078-8090-6

Contents

Preface and Acknowledgments

This book is the culmination of several years of study of the early works of the poet Rainer Maria Rilke, beginning with a dissertation on *Buch der Bilder* which was completed in 1969 at the University of Pennsylvania. The significance of these early works as the basis for the overall development of Rilke's creativity has become increasingly clear as this project has progressed, and it is hoped that this study will succeed in filling a noticeable lacuna in the body of knowledge about this period of the poet's life.

Portions of Chapters Two, Three, and Five have appeared previously. The editors of *The Centennial Review*, *Orbis Litterarum*, and Suhrkamp Verlag have kindly granted permission to use material published under their auspices.

The right to reproduce J. Toorop's "Maiden with Swans" (p. iv) has been given by the Rijksmuseum, Amsterdam; H. Vogeler's "Undine" (p. 24) by the Worpsweder Archiv, Worpswede; Rodin's "The Age of Bronze" (p. 43) by the Musée Rodin, Paris; F. Hodler's "Spring" (p. 97) by the Museum Folkwang, Essen; and G. Klimt's "Portrait of Adele Bloch-Bauer" (p. 115) by the Österreichische Galerie, Vienna.

I would like here to express my appreciation to the University of Houston for its assistance in this project in the form of an Initiation Grant in 1970 and a Limited Grant-In-Aid in 1973 and to the American Council of Learned Societies, the Deutscher Akademischer Austauschdienst, and the AATG, grants from which permitted me to spend the summer of 1973 conducting research in Germany. I wish also to express my thanks to my colleagues Gertrud Pickar and Harold Lenz whose suggestions and careful reading of the manuscript have been of inestimable worth to me. To my wife, Deanna, I owe a special debt of gratitude for her patience, support, and encouragement.

*   *   *

Houston, January 1977   K. E. W.

I. Introduction

As one of the most important and influential as well as one of the most enigmatic poets of our century, Rainer Maria Rilke has engendered a long list of scholarly studies designed to clarify the many aspects of his life and works. There is, for example, a host of works dealing with the poet's relationship with other poets, the effect of certain places, countries or peoples upon his writing, and no less impressive, the effect of certain works of art and certain artists on his development. The poet remained throughout his life highly sensitive to outside influences which often provided him with just the needed impetus or inspiration to move forward with his work, or they reinforced in him tendencies which were already present in his personality. These studies, therefore, have contributed measurably to the understanding of Rilke's personality and his writing, and it is now clear that the years in Paris, Italy, and Spain contributed profoundly to the unique qualities which were his, as did his stay in Russia and in Scandinavia and his amazingly varied associations with the intelligentsia of Europe.

Of all these studies, none have been more productive for an understanding of the poet and his works than those dealing with his relationship with the art and artists of his time. We have now become aware, for example, that Paul Cézanne, Auguste Rodin, and even Paul Klee and Pablo Picasso[1] had something basic to do with the form of Rilke's thinking and writing during certain vital periods of his life, and we have begun to sense that the poet almost invariably turned to the fine arts or to specific artists for direction in his most serious crises. Rilke was extremely impressionable with regard to art and astonishingly perceptive in his understanding of its fundamental qualities and goals. The investigation of the poet's concern with art has been especially fruitful, for it has not only contributed to basic knowledge about Rilke, but has also frequently given insight into the significance and value of the works of art or the artists themselves with whom he had contact.

It is surprising, therefore, that Rilke's involvement with art during his earlier years, particularly with the German *Jugendstil*, has until now received very little attention in Rilke scholarship. These were the years, after all, in which much of his fundamental development occurred and in which he formulated many of his most important concepts about life and art. Yet except for some general references to the poet's association

1

and involvement in this movement, a brief article or two, and an unpublished dissertation, this subject has remained almost untouched.

Bert Herzog, in what is undoubtedly the most perceptive piece on Rilke's *Jugendstil* involvement,[2] limits his discussion to a very general reference to the "Boticelli-atmosphere" of Rilke's early works, to the poet's use of precious and unusual words, and to the underlying melancholia which prevails. He specifically refers to Rilke's associations with Lou Andreas-Salomé and the Munich circle of *Jugendstil* artists and draws attention to several poems in the *Stunden-Buch* collection which were written as a result of that association. Finally, he addresses himself to the religious tone of *Stunden-Buch*, calling it a "theology of *Jugendstil*,"[3] and finds such a tone to be typical for all of Rilke's early works. Claude David in an excellent article about Stefan George[4] makes only brief references to Rilke's associations with *Jugendstil* in order to support his contention that many major poets, including George himself of course, were heavily influenced by the art of the time. Paul Requadt[5] dedicates a section of his chapter on Rilke and Italy to the poet's early flirtations with *Jugendstil* and establishes the fact that Rilke's entire concept of the Italian Renaissance was colored by his association with that movement and with the ideas of art as they were pursued by the earlier Pre-Raphaelites. Requadt also points out that some of Rilke's major themes, the maidens for example or the tension between the intellectual forces and the primordial drives, found their impetus in the poet's *Jugendstil* affiliations in Munich.

The most thorough treatment of Rilke and *Jugendstil* is an unpublished dissertation by Marieluise Champagne[6] in which the author presents a wide variety of interesting biographical material about Rilke's connections with the art and artists of the period. She makes us aware of the poet's interest in the developments in the Liberty House in London, of his personal associations with the various artists in Munich and Berlin, and of his fascination with the works of Jens Peter Jacobsen and Maurice Maeterlinck who in her opinion also demonstrated strong predilections for *Jugendstil*-like themes and motifs. Champagne then undertakes an extended discussion of some of Rilke's *Jugendstil* themes and motifs such as his treatment of "silence" and "vitalism." Despite the very useful biographical information and the attempt at a detailed thematic discussion, however, the results of Champagne's dissertation are unsatisfactory. For example, her concept of literary *Jugendstil* is much too broad, and that forces her to include an entire spectrum of themes which often have very little to do with the period in question. The general lack of organization within the study contributes further to the problem of clarity. But the work's most serious flaw is its failure to come to terms adequately with Rilke's most striking and important contribution to *Jugendstil*, namely his poetic style.

It is my purpose in the present study to enlarge upon the sometimes useful but inadequate information already available and to provide a systematic investigation of Rilke's impressive involvement with the art and artists of the *Jugendstil* movement. Thus it is hoped that the origin and motivation of many of his unique characteristics might more clearly come into focus and that perhaps also in the process a greater understanding may be found for the art of this period, particularly as it is considered from the perspective of the poet's own view.

Before beginning our study, it seems necessary to sketch the essential qualities of *Jugendstil*, particularly those elements which will form the basis of our discussion. As the later German counterpart of the European movement generally designated as *Art Nouveau*, *Jugendstil* flourished briefly but intensely from about 1894 to 1904. Although it developed some years later than elsewhere in Europe, it adopted most of the primary goals and concepts of the movement at large while adding, of course, several unique features of its own which arose primarily from its German heritage and background. In Darmstadt, Dresden, Munich, Berlin, and Vienna, the movement's main centers, provocative exhibitions were organized and influential schools founded. New periodicals sprang up in order to proclaim the theories and reproduce the works of the artists gathered under the rubric of *Jugendstil*, and through these periodicals, the tenets of the new movement became widely known and debated. Its major figures, Peter Behrens, Hermann Obrist, August Endell, Gustav Klimt, Heinrich Vogeler, and others, eventually became famous and were called upon to contribute to the most important artistic ventures of the time. These artists sought to create with their works, as had their forerunners elsewhere in Europe, a new art form which they felt would be free of the "vulgarity" of Naturalism and the "lifelessness" of *Historismus*, the two prevailing styles in Germany in those years. They wanted to liberate nature and their art from the traditional limitations set by objective portrayal in order, they hoped, to reveal what they believed was the true inner reality and harmony of life.

The themes of the works of *Jugendstil* reflect these goals. The world, as it was protrayed in the art of the movement, is a subjective one based on fantasy, dream, or fairy tale, and populated by innocent, dancing maidens, dashing young knights, or mysterious water sprites. It is an artistic realm where a quiet and delicate beauty reigns, where the harsh and blunt realities of "secular" life find no place. It is often the scene of a softly decaying park with quiescent ponds, shimmering swans, and verdant water lilies. The works of the period convey a hushed and exquisite ambience, and the subtlety of gesture, stance, or facial expression indicate the work's essential emotional tone. In addition, there is inherent in all of these works an underlying tension created by the polarities and dichotomies of life which these artists acutely felt within themselves and within their age. In their works, this tension sometimes takes the form of a contrast between a feeling of over-refinement and resignation and an undercurrent of primordial drives, or perhaps in the confrontation of the innocence and naiveté of a young maiden with her newly awakened erotic passions.

The style is even more recognizable and unique than the themes, for it was here that the artists really tried to make their break with tradition. In an attempt to enliven and rejuvenate their art, they chose the now characteristic, strongly curved, organic line which endowed the works with an effect of movement and rhythmical energy. Using a technique inspired by Japanese and to some extent medieval art, the artists also composed their works in a series of flat surface planes which eliminated all perception of depth, foreground or background, and revealed a new and unexpected harmony within the work. The artists of *Jugendstil* exhibited a strong preference for ornateness and decoration and chose for their works the most costly materials, including precious metals and woods. They branched out from the traditional forms of painting and sculpture and became remarkably skilled in silversmithing, tapestry weaving, book illustrating, and interior decorating, all of which they placed on an equal artistic basis with the more traditional fine arts. Perhaps as their ultimate attempt at inner harmony, some of these artists often designed individual rooms or even entire buildings in which each piece of furniture, the wall coverings, every light fixture, and even the dimensions of the rooms themselves had to fit into their unified and harmonious scheme.

The movement was, of course, rather short-lived. This may partially be attributed to the fact of its wide acceptance and eventual popularization and distortion through mass consumption. Its break with artistic tradition in regard to compositional techniques and artistic perspective, however, and the creative impulse that it represented had a lasting effect on the development of much of the modern art which followed.

Because of the multiplicity of attributes, the ties with the past, and the affinities with the future, the study of *Jugendstil* art and literature has experienced a varied and uneven history.[7] In the years immediately following its demise, the years in which expressionism and later the *Bauhaus* reigned, *Jugendstil* stood in great disfavor as the embodiment of a tired and decadent bourgeois art. It was only in the late twenties and early thirties, and then very tenuously, that an occasional student of the period, such as Fritz Schmalenbach[8] and Ernst Michalski,[9] began to take a closer look at *Jugendstil*. They discovered in retrospect that the movement represented the first quiet but significant revolt against a total dependence on the naturalistic viewpoint and that some of the characteristics and techniques, especially the two-dimensional composition and the Nietzschean vitalism, formed the basis upon which many later artists were to build their art. Other scholars, such as Dolf Sternberger,[10] continued to underscore the decadent qualities of the movement, but even their concern with the period drew additional attention to its existence so that the importance of *Jugendstil* art became more and more evident with the years.

During the fifties and sixties, then, a series of important studies appeared which precipitated a general rebirth of interest in the period and a recognition of its pivotal importance for the development of modern art forms. Perhaps the most influential of these is a book by Tschudi Madsen.[11] In his study, Madsen attempts a comprehensive, albeit brief history of the many aspects of the movement in its broad European and American context. He discusses its antecedents in Pre-Raphaelite art and its assimilation of certain traits of medieval and oriental architecture and painting. He also draws distinctions between the various manifestations of the style as they occurred in France, Belgium, America, Scotland, Spain, Italy, Germany, and Austria. In what amounts to his main thesis, Madsen maintains that the ultimate importance of the movement rests with its attention to the applied arts so that these creative forms henceforth enjoyed renewed respect and devotion among the arts. Hans Hofstätter,[12] in contrast, emphasizes only the fine arts in his book. He too underscores the international perspective, although he attributes more significance to the German phase of the movement than does Madsen. Hofstätter also considers the art of the period on the basis of the traditions from which it sprang and includes in his discussion the influence it exercised upon the art which was to follow. If he can be faulted in any way, it is that he tends to broaden the concept of *Jugendstil* too much so as to include artists as dissimilar as Gauguin and Modersohn-Becker on the one hand and Bonnard and Matisse on the other. A shorter, though no less influential study of *Jugendstil* was undertaken by the eminent critic Wolfdietrich Rasch.[13] In his essay, Rasch addresses himself first to an investigation of the development of art at the turn of the century from impressionism to neo-impressionism and finally to *Jugendstil* itself. He detects similarities in the pointillism and two-dimensionality of Seurat's works, for example, and those of van de Velde. The most important contribution of this essay, however, is Rasch's analysis of the artistic theories upon which the art of the period was based. From concepts found in the various theoretical works, Rasch asserts that the *Jugendstil* artists consciously sought to redefine and to realize in their creativity a certain unifying and enlivening *Lebensstrom* or "life's force" which they felt permeated all aspects of life, a force, however, which they believed had been denied or ignored by artistic trends of recent times. The two-dimensionality of their composition and their highly curved, organic lines, according to Rasch, were an attempt at symbolically demonstrating the *Lebensstrom* and recreating its harmonious effect within the work of art.

While art historians were becoming increasingly interested in *Jugendstil*, many literary scholars began to see similar qualities in the literary production of the period. The result is a series of works investigating what has now become known as literary *Jugendstil*. The first of these works is an unpublished dissertation by Elisabeth Klein[14] in which the first catalogue of *Jugendstil* themes in German poetry is undertaken. Although this work is certainly not a definitive study on the topic, it nevertheless provided the impetus for much of the work that was to follow. A far more sophisticated approach, though only a short article, is Volker Klotz's "Jugendstil in der Lyrik"[15] which appeared in 1957, the same year as Miss Klein's dissertation. Klotz adheres very closely in his analysis of the lyrical style of the period to models taken from *Jugendstil* art. He ignores for the most part typical themes of *Jugendstil* and concentrates on stylistic and structural equivalents in the poetry. He pays particular attention, for example, to the significance of the use of participles and adjectives, and he emphasizes the importance of the decorative qualities of the language in general.

In the ensuing years, several other major works appeared, each defining more precisely one aspect or the other of literary *Jugendstil*. Jost Hermand, who is probably the most prolific and certainly one of the most articulate scholars in this area, published his perceptive essay on *Jugendstil* lyric in 1964.[16] Hermand emphasizes in his work the sense of alienation which the *Jugendstil* writers experienced vis-à-vis the common and often crass surroundings of the modern technological world and their desire to flee from such a world into an exquisite and luxurious realm of their own creation. He also points to a type of carnival atmosphere which is incorporated into some of the lyrics—a playfulness in sound and rhythm, for example, and an almost desperate flight from reality into fantasy and frivolity. Edelgard Hajek[17] takes a rather skeptical look at the whole process of adapting the thematic and structural elements of the art of the period to the corresponding literature. Quite properly, she discounts many of the apparent similarities as purely superficial and inconsequential. This is particularly true in some discussions of theme where the mere appearance of a swan or a lily pad has provided the excuse for a literary comparison. There is, nevertheless, a genuine form of literary *Jugendstil*, according to Hajek, but it occurs only where specific stylistic devices are utilized which create the same or similar effect within the individual medium of expression. In the final section of her work, she proceeds then to demonstrate what she believes to be some of the genuine characteristics of literary *Jugendstil*. Although the conclusion of the book proves quite useful, particularly as a study of Oscar Wilde's *Salomé*, the real impact of Hajek's study lies in the penetrating questions she asks and the corrective effect these questions exercise on the thinking about the period.

As a rapid overview of the scholarship of literary *Jugendstil*, Dominik Jost's small volume in the Metzler series serves a very useful function.[18] He begins his work with a detailed definition of terms based primarily on concepts developed by Klein, Klotz, Hermand and others and then devotes his attention to a bibliographical catalogue of the various studies dealing with *Jugendstil* qualities in, for example, the works of Nietzsche, George, Hofmannsthal, Thomas Mann, Wedekind, and Rilke. In the final section of his book, Jost presents a series of literary passages from the poetry of Dauthendey, Lasker-Schüler, Stadler, Eduard Stucken and others that he considers typical of *Jugendstil*. Jost Hermand's anthology of essays[19] gives an overview of a different but no less valuable sort in that he republishes the most important documents of *Jugendstil* scholarship both in the arts and in literature. His own essays as well as those of Sternberger, Schmalenbach, Klotz, David, Herzog, Rasch, etc. are included. The reader may be astonished to find such a variety and abundance of serious scholarly investigations into a phenomenon which for so long was regarded with derision. It is clear from Hermand's anthology and from the specialized works about other aspects of the movement, which we have been unable to include in the discussion here, that *Jugendstil* art and literature have become not only a popular subject among scholars but an important one as well for a better understanding of the complex and intriguing period at the beginning of our century.

II. Rilke and Jugendstil

Rilke's relationship to the art and artists of *Jugendstil* extended beyond the influence of the *Zeitgeist* or the sharing of general intellectual and emotional concerns with one's contemporaries, for he became actively involved as a critic and as a participant in the movement. He knew personally many of the artists involved, was knowledgeable about the works of many more, and was vividly aware of the theories upon which the art of the whole period was based. His profound interest and involvement grew from the fact that, as was so often the case in his life, he perceived in works of a different medium a basic similarity to his own thoughts, emotions, and artistic goals. There was nothing startling or incomprehensible to him in these works, for they expressed many of his own deepest desires and concerns. As his association with the movement increased and as his understanding deepened, the art of *Jugendstil* served more and more as a reinforcement or as an impetus for the crystallization of inherent tendencies in Rilke himself.[1]

Rilke's general enthusiasm for the fine arts became evident in Munich for the first time, although he had demonstrated even in Prague an inclination in that direction. When in 1896, at the age of twenty-one, he moved to the Bavarian capital, he soon found himself caught up in the numerous social and artistic activities to be found there. Under the guidance of his illustrious companion of those days, Lou Andreas-Salomé, and a circle of her close friends who gathered periodically outside Munich in Wolfratshausen, Rilke began his first intensive study of art. He became acquainted not only with the works of the past such as art from the Italian Renaissance but also with works being produced in his own time. The latter included, of course, the art of *Jugendstil*. During these years, 1896–1897, the movement was becoming more generally known and very popular in Munich. Both of its periodicals, *Jugend* and *Simplicissimus*, were founded in 1896 and began publishing their famous essays on modern art and culture. The journals also established new art forms in their illustrations, caricatures, and reproductions. In 1897, one of the most important art exhibitions in the development of *Jugendstil* was held in the Glaspalast in Munich where the applied arts were displayed alongside paintings and sculpture and accepted as equals. In addition to the representative works of over thirty *Jugendstil* artists including such figures as Behrens, Leistikow, Pankok, Obrist, Th. Th.

Heine, Riemerschmid, Eckmann, and Endell, there were two special rooms completely decorated in *Jugendstil*. The exhibition caused a great stir among the various art circles in Munich including those with which the young Rilke had contact.

In two letters written in August, 1897, Rilke comments enthusiastically and at length about his impressions of the exhibition, and his statements testify to the sympathy with which he viewed the goals of *Jugendstil* and to his feelings about the movement's unique qualities. He praises Munich, for example, as the fertile soil from which the young artists derived strength and growth, and he believes that their tendency toward decorativeness found its impetus in Munich as well:

Ich habe die Empfindung, daß man das Dekorative das neuen Stils, insoweit es in München seine Wiege hat und durch Otto Eckmann, Hermann Obrist, August Endell etc. vertreten wird, nur verstehen kann, wenn man einerseits dieses Milieu, andererseits die Einflüsse kennen gelernt hat, welche es auf die Menschen, besonders auf die Schaffenden ausübt.[2]*

Rilke also recognizes the rebirth of the applied arts and the founding of a new style which he hopes would make inroads into the world of art: "Sobald es einmal so weit ist, daß wir unsere Stuben nicht mehr im anempfundenen Geschmack vergangener Epochen einrichten, wird diese Wiederbelebung des Kunstgewerbes uns von großer Bedeutung sein" (SW V, 323).† He realizes furthermore the important influence of English and Japanese art in the revolutionary lines of the new style and the effect these lines will have in the further development of the applied arts:

Die Engländer und Japaner haben uns den Wert der "Linie" wieder schätzen gelehrt, und die Anwendung dieser Kenntnis wird dann die Form unserer Möbel und die Zeichnung der Stoffe bestimmen. Die Wiedergewinnung der "Linie" hat es auch mit sich gebracht, daß die graphischen Künste in vollstem Umfange gepflegt werden, und ihre Ausnützung für die Illustration und Ausschmückung der Bücher und zur Ausführung von Plakatanschlägen hat der Kunst einen neuen, breiten Weg zum Verständnis der Menge gewiesen (SW V, 323).‡

* "I have the impression that the decorative nature of the new style, in that it was born in Munich and is represented by Otto Eckmann, Hermann Obrist, August Endell etc., can only be understood if one has gotten to know this milieu and the influence it has had on the people, particularly those who create."[3]

† "As soon as we have got to the point of no longer decorating our rooms in the adopted taste of past eras, this rejuvenation of the applied arts will have great meaning for us."

‡ "The English and the Japanese have taught us to value the 'line' again, and the application of this knowledge will determine the style of our furniture and the design of our materials. The revitalization of the "line" has also brought about a renewed interest in

In all of his analytical comments, Rilke does not overlook the important role played by *Jugend* and *Simplicissimus* in providing an opportunity for the young artists to make their works known:

Zwei Zeitschriften sind es vor allem, welche der modernen Griffelkunst neben dem modernen Schrifttum gleichberechtigt Raum gewähren wollen,—auch dann, wenn sie selbständig und nicht eigentlich als Illustration auftritt. Die "Jugend" und der "Simplicissimus", beide in München erscheinend, fördern eine Reihe von Künstlern, dadurch, daß sie ihren Arbeiten einen entsprechend günstigen Platz und Verbreitung verschaffen und ihnen in ihren literarischen Beiträgen Anregung und die Gelegenheit bieten, sich in der eigentlichen Textkunst, den Kopfleisten und Zierrändern und Vignetten zu versuchen (SW V, 327).*

All of these statements point to the poet's thorough familiarity with the qualities of the art of the time, its origins, and its goals.

Rilke's association with the *Jugendstil* in Munich went further, however, than just a general familiarity derived from visiting exhibitions and participating in discussions of art. He had firsthand knowledge of the movement through his close friend Emil Orlik (1870–1932) whom he had met first in Prague in 1896. Orlik, by his study of Japanese art forms and English and Scottish painters and by his utilization of their techniques in his works, became not only in Munich but also later in Vienna and Berlin one of the promising young representatives of *Jugendstil*. He is particularly remembered for his illustrations of Lafcadio Hearn's many books on Japan.

Rilke had an opportunity to observe Orlik's development during this period, and although he was not yet as perceptive an observer as he later became, he nevertheless absorbed and comprehended much that Orlik undertook to accomplish. In an essay, "Ein Prager Künstler," which was written two years after Rilke left Munich and published in 1900 in *Ver sacrum*, Rilke demonstrated his understanding of Orlik's works. In one especially indicative passage, for example, which is remarkably similar to statements made by the most recent critics of *Jugendstil*,[4] Rilke comments on Orlik's attempt to extract his subjects from their arbitrary

---

the graphic arts which are now pursued to the fullest extent, and their utilization for book illustration and decoration and for posters have provided for the masses a new and accessible way toward an understanding of art."

* "Above all, there are two periodicals that desire to give equal attention to modern writing as well as to the modern art of engraving—even when it appears entirely independent and not actually as an illustration. *Jugend* and *Simplicissimus*, both published in Munich, promote a whole series of artists in that they provide a suitable place for publication and proper circulation for these artists' works and in the actual literary texts give them the opportunity of trying out their skills at text–art, illumination and vignettes."

and common environment and place them in a new but more universal and lasting context:

Aus allen Wandlungen und Wirrnissen und Übergängen soll die Kunst den "Extrakt der Dinge", welcher ihre Seele ist, retten; sie soll jedes einzelne Ding isolieren aus dem zufälligen Nebeneinander heraus, um es in die größeren Zusammenhänge einzuschalten, längs welcher die Ereignisse, die wirklichen Ereignisse, sich vollziehen. Dies ist der Inhalt von Orliks Streben auch, und es scheint mir eine ernste Künstlerabsicht zu sein (SW V, 474–75).*

Rilke's conception of the *Jugendstil* artist's attempt at creating a more comprehensive and revealing harmony in his works through new and revolutionary compositional techniques is readily apparent from this passage.

In October, 1897, Rilke left Munich, accompanied by Lou Andreas-Salomé, and moved to Berlin. While there, he began a formal study of art history at the university, and although he often neglected his studies to write and to participate in the social events of the city, his interest in the art of *Jugendstil* only grew in intensity. After a visit to one of the well-known galleries in Berlin at the time, the Kunsthandlung Keller & Reiner, Rilke wrote an essay, "Die neue Kunst in Berlin," in which he confirms his enthusiasm once more for the art of *Jugendstil* and expresses particularly his admiration for the work of the celebrated *Jugendstil* painter, interior decorator, artisan, architect, and theorist, Henry van de Velde (1863–1957), who had decorated part of the gallery. In a description of one of van de Velde's rooms, Rilke finds it very difficult to suppress his excitement over the visual spectacle he found there:

Torfüllungen, Vitrinen, Tische, alles in hellem Holz, leicht, ruhig, gesund. Alle Bewegung breites Wellenschlagen, ein rhythmischer Ausgleich von Last und Kraft. Nirgends Hast, nirgends Angst. Wie in festen Angeln schwingt die Bewegung. Und sie wiederholt sich freier und leichter oben im Fries. Die Farbe macht alle Dinge verwandt und giebt dem Raum eine einheitliche Selbstverständlichkeit; man vergißt fast die Einzelheiten zu betrachten, so sehr dienen sie alle einträchtig dem Ganzen. Die Organisation ist bewundernswert. Nirgends wird Kraft verschwendet. . . . Jede Linie lebt sich aus (SW V, 443–44).†

---

* "From all the alterations, confusion, and transformations, art ought to be able to save the 'essence of things,' which is its very soul; it ought to be able to isolate each individual thing from its arbitrary environment in order to place it in the larger context in which events, the real events, take place. That is also the basis for Orlik's work, and it appears to me to be a serious artistic endeavor."

† "The carvings on the doors, the display cases, the tables, everything in light wood, delicate, peaceful, whole. All movement a series of broad waves breaking, a rhythmical equalization of weight and strength. Nowhere haste, nowhere anxiety. The movement revolves as on solid axes, and it is repeated more freely and delicately above in the frieze.

In a further evaluation of the Belgian's work, an evaluation strikingly similar to his remarks about Emil Orlik, Rilke praises van de Velde's knowledge of his material and his ability to allow each creation to reach its full potential:

Von allen, welche den Dingen zu sich selber helfen, begreift sie keiner so wie *Van der Velde* [sic]. Er kennt sie alle ganz genau und weiß ihre heimlichsten Wünsche. Er hat die echte Liebe zu ihnen: er verzärtelt sie nicht, er erzieht sie. Sie sollen nicht Müßige werden. Er will sie stark und still und arbeitsam. Er neigt sich zu jedem: "Was willst du werden?" Und dann läßt er es einfach reifen und schützt es nur, daß es in Schönheit werde (SW V, 443).*

Rilke's admiration for van de Velde's ability to work with things and materials touches on one of his own overriding obsessions of the time and underscores the close affinity which he felt for the artists of this movement.

Besides his general familiarity with the *Jugendstil* works that were displayed in various art galleries of Berlin, Rilke, as in Munich, also came to know in detail the works of several of the major artists of the movement. Among these was Ludwig von Hofmann (1861–1945) to whom Rilke felt particularly attracted. Von Hofmann's works repeatedly treat the figures of young boys and girls at play, dancing, bathing, or resting in an innocent, dream-like paradise in which they are apparently oblivious to the world of passion or reality. In typical *Jugendstil* fashion, these figures are usually portrayed in an arabesque manner, wreathed in gauze veils and silhouetted against the sky like the young, willowy trees that form the background. Many of Rilke's early works, as we shall later see, incorporate these very same characteristics, and we realize once more the basis for the poet's attraction.

This similarity in artistic interests led to the first occasion in Rilke's life where he directly collaborated with a *Jugendstil* artist. In 1898, a series of poems by Rilke entitled *Lieder der Mädchen* (SW I, 172–81) appeared in *Pan*, accompanied by two specially commissioned sketches by von Hofmann. These thirteen poems are perfectly matched in topic and

---

The color relates all objects and lends a unifying self-evidence to the room; one almost forgets to notice the individual objects, they serve the entirety so harmoniously. The organizational plan is admirable. In no instance is energy wasted. . . . Each line lives its life to the fullest."

* "Of all those who assist objects in their self-realization, none comprehends the process as does *Van der Velde* [sic]. He knows them all thoroughly and recognizes their most secret desires. He possesses a genuine love for them: he does not pamper them, he trains them. They are not allowed to be lazy. He wants them to be strong, quiet, and diligent. He nods to each of them: 'What do you want to become?' And then he allows each to develop simply and protects each so that it will be fulfilled in beauty."

tone by the illustrations of the *Jugendstil* artist. In the one sketch, the young girls exude in their dance a carefree, innocent air with their slender figures almost untouched by desire (see illus. 2). In the other, however, a young girl, alone with her emotions, is torn by unknown, erotic sensations which are symbolized by two ominous shadows in the background and reinforced by the swirling lines of the grass and the trees.

Later, Rilke reversed the process and attempted, probably for the first time in his career, to write poems inspired by an existing work of art. He composed a series of fourteen poems entitled "Die Bilder entlang" (SW III, 621–28), which he based on sketches by von Hofmann that had earlier appeared in *Pan*. In these poems, he tried to capture the theme, the atmosphere, and the technique of the artist. With titles such as "Swanlake," "Kissing Pair," "Reverie," and "Longing," the poems depict the typical subjects of von Hofmann's world and attempt to incorporate in form the characteristic pronounced lines, strong rhythm, and exaggerated gestures of his works as well. During the same period, Rilke also wrote a short sketch entitled "Spiel," which he dedicated to Ludwig von Hofmann. The remarks in the preface indicate his esteem:

Lieber Ludwig von Hofmann,
In der Erinnerung sind mir Ihre Bilder wie Freuden und wie Geschenke. Oft wünschte ich Ihnen dessen ein Zeichen zu geben. Keine Gelegenheit kam. Bis mir dieses Lied gelang, das einmal später in einem Buch, "SPIELE," stehen soll. Mir ist, als könnten Sie es lieb haben und meine Liebe dafür so vermehren. Nur Sie. Darum reiche ich es Ihnen, Ludwig von Hofmann zu eigen (SW III, 376).*

This direct correlation between Rilke's works and the new art continued for the next few years to play a very prominent role in the poet's creativity.

His sojourn in Berlin was interrupted by two trips to Russia and thereafter by a six-week stay in Worpswede, both of which continued and even increased his artistic and personal ties to the *Jugendstil* movement. Rilke first went to Russia on 25 April 1899, accompanied by Lou Andreas-Salomé and her husband Professor Andreas. As the daughter of a Russian general, Lou had long spoken to Rilke about the attractions of the open Russian countryside and the simple and pious Russian people, and the poet became eager to see what she described for himself. That first trip, unfortunately, was limited to a week in Moscow and

---

* "Dear Ludwig von Hofmann: Your pictures are a gift and a joy to me. I have often desired to present a token of appreciation to you. There was no opportunity until I was successful in this *Lied* which will one day appear in a book of 'Scenes.' To me it seems that you might like it and thereby increase my own love for it. Only you could do that. For this reason, I am giving it to you, Ludwig von Hofmann, in dedication."

2. *Ludwig von Hofmann: "Maidens"* (Pan, 4, 4[1898], 209)

six weeks in St. Petersburg, but Rilke did have the opportunity of meeting Tolstoy very briefly. He also met several other Russian artists and poets[5] and spent considerable time in the art museums of those cities.

Rilke felt dissatisfied by his first trip and began immediately thereafter to prepare for a second one. A year later, in May, 1900, after having studied some Russian language, history, and culture, he again set out, once more in the company of Lou, to explore the vast reaches of the Russian steppes. This time, he fully intended to penetrate to the heart of this mysterious land and discover, if possible, its very "soul." He did get as far as Yasnaya Polyana, Tolstoy's country estate, where he had gone to re-establish his acquaintance with the old writer, and he did spend a few days in a peasant village and a few days with the folk poet Drojin. Otherwise, he again confined his activities to the more sophisticated and cultured centers of the major cities. He nevertheless felt gratified this time by his experiences and upon his return believed that he had truly come to understand the essence of Russian life.

From his comments at the time, it is clear that what Rilke saw of Russia, of its countryside and its people, confirmed in his mind the preconceptions which he had formed under the influence of Lou, preconceptions which were decidedly typical of the thinking of the *Jugendstil* period. This land, in Rilke's eyes, represented a type of utopia where, despite the threats of the modern machine age, life, men, and art had retained an original purity, vitality, and unity. The serfs, in their simple piety and naive innocence, he believed, lived in complete harmony with their surroundings, the soil, and the universal forces of life and knew and respected the real essence of all being: a belief which was, of course, essential to the thinking of *Jugendstil*. The art of the people, as incorporated in the icons and the churches, reflected this inner harmony as well, and was worthy therefore of the greatest respect and emulation. In contrast, his own age and even his own existence seemed artificial and all too separated from the essence of life. As a result, the Russian serfs and the Russian countryside became for Rilke the symbolic embodiment of all his artistic and personal aspirations and a new source for his inspiration.

Rilke, however, did not overlook the more recent art and artists of Russia in his enthusiasm for its people, as his two essays, "Russische Kunst" and "Moderne russische Kunstbestrebungen" (both written in Westerwede in 1901), will attest. Again, he attributed to them qualities which were also vital to the *Jugendstil*. In both of these rather subjective essays, it becomes evident that Rilke discerned in the more recent developments of the art and in the works of individual artists the same harmony and unity with the folk spirit and with the forces of life which

he had recognized in the older icons and church murals. With reference to the famous painter Viktor Vasnetsov, one of the most important members of the so-called "Wanderers" or Manontov group (who were only on the periphery of what might objectively be considered the Russian *Art Nouveau*), Rilke writes: "Er kehrte eilig nach Rußland zurüch [von Rom] und begann 1885 das bedeutende Werk, welches ein glänzendes Zeugnis wurde für die Lebendigkeit des russischen Gottes und die tiefe, aus dem Leben strömende Frömmigkeit des Meisters" (SW V, 501–02).*
In a further passage, he continues:

Auch sein Streben ist es, die Kunst mit der russischen Seele zu verbinden, Kanäle zu graben, ein System von Kanälen, das ihre dunklen, glänzenden Gewässer hinausführt in die Kunst. Schlichter als die anderen, demütiger als sie, wagt er nicht an *seine* Seele dabei zu denken; er sucht die große, gemeinsame Seele des Volkes auf, sucht sie im Leben der Bauern, in ihren Gebräuchen, in ihrem Glauben und Aberglauben, in ihren uralten Liedern, den Bylinen. . . . Er hat das Heidentum dieser Seele erforscht und ihre Frömmigkeit. Er hat sich von ihr in die Kirchen führen lassen, vor die alten, nachgedunkelten Ikone, vor denen seit Jahrhunderten die Menschen beten und die Kerzen brennen (SW V, 618–19).†

Vasnetsov's "inner piety," his "comprehension of the Russian God" and the "Russian soul," and his attempts at capturing in his art the harmony and unity of the essential forces of life, as Rilke describes them in these passages, combine some of the very qualities for which the artists of the *Jugendstil* were striving, and for which Rilke himself was striving. The poet's attribution of these qualities to Vasnetsov and his works clearly indicates the perspective from which he viewed current Russian art. This art was an example to him, as had been the art of Henry van de Velde and Ludwig von Hofmann, of characteristics he was determined to realize in his own creativity.

In addition, Rilke was not unaware of the influence that European *Art Nouveau* specifically had had on recent Russian art. In his second essay, he makes mention of the latest group of artists who had been to Paris and other European capitals and had been exposed to the works of

* "He hurriedly returned to Russia [from Rome], and began in 1885 his important work which became a splendid testimony to the vitality of the Russian God and of the deep piety, streaming forth from life, of the master."

† "It is also his goal to combine art with the Russian soul, to dig canals, a system of canals, that leads their dark, splendid waters to his art. Simpler than the others, more humble than they, he dares not think of *his* soul in this process; he searches for the great, common soul of the people, searches for it in the life of the peasants, in their customs, their beliefs and superstitions, in their age-old songs, in the Byliny. . . . He has investigated the heathenism of this soul and its piety. He has been led by it to the churches, to the old icons grown dark with age before which people for centuries have prayed and candles have burned."

the leading artists of *Art Nouveau*. Returning to the soil of Mother Russia, these artists created then their own brand of *Jugendstil* which preserved an essential harmony with the Russian soul:

Aber auch die Generation, welche jetzt aufsteigt, ist in Paris gewesen. Das sind welterfahrene, wissende junge Leute von überaus feinem Geschmack und tiefer Bildung. . . . Sie haben die Impressionisten, die Neo-Impressionisten, die Pointillisten und alle neuen Bestrebungen erlebt, sie kennen die Radierungen Klingers und die Bilder Segantinis, sie haben das Musée Gustave Moreau in der rue de La Rochefoucauld besucht, haben manches von Rodin gesehen und Beardsley auf sich wirken lassen, und nach alldem sind sie mit ungestörtem Gleichgewicht nach Hause und zu ihrer Arbeit zurückgekehrt. Von Zeit zu Zeit erscheinen sie auf unseren Ausstellungen und schon hat man angefangen, sich einige Namen zu merken. Sjerow, Maljawin, Konstantin Somow, Konstantin Korowin, Alexander Benois sind die bekanntesten (SW V, 620–21).*

Finally, the poet is careful not to forget that, in Russia too, the applied arts were enjoying a rebirth of importance and that the most prominent artists had begun to be interested, as were the *Jugendstil* artists of Western Europe, in making handcrafted furniture, painting tiles, weaving wall hangings, and illustrating books.

Years later, Rilke continued to claim that the Russian experience was the most important of his life, which is an exaggeration no doubt. It did, however, lead directly to the creation of several of his important works—*Geschichten vom lieben Gott*, major portions of *Stunden-Buch*, and many of the most prominent *Jugendstil* poems in *Buch der Bilder*. More important for our study is the fact that the Russian experience served as a vital reinforcement of Rilke's growing attachment to the *Jugendstil* movement.

Despite the profound effects of the Russian trips for Rilke's development, it was really in Worpswede that his involvement with the *Jugendstil* reached its apotheosis. The poet arrived there on 22 August 1900, shortly after his return from Russia, at the invitation of Heinrich Vogeler. The two had met previously in 1898 in Florence where Rilke had gone to study the Renaissance and Vogeler to spend a short holiday.

---

* "But this generation too, which is now becoming prominent, has been to Paris. These are sophisticated, knowledgeable young people with exceptionally refined tastes and thorough education. . . . They have experienced the Impressionists, the Neo-Impressionists, the Pointillists as well as other new movements, they know the etchings of Klinger and Segantini's pictures, they have visited the Musée Gustave Moreau on the rue de La Rochefoucauld, have studied various things of Rodin and have subjected themselves to the impressions of Beardsley, and after all this, they have returned home to their work with an undisturbed sense of proportion. From time to time, they appear in our exhibitions, and we have already begun to note a few of their names. Sjerov, Maljavin, Konstantin Somov, Konstantin Korovin, Alexander Benois are the best known."

During this time, Vogeler's friend, Rudolf Borchardt, who was also an acquaintance of Rilke's, took the artist to meet the poet. Vogeler's description of the poet's way of life indicates Rilke's early attraction to the unusual and exotic—tendencies which played a major role in the lives of many of the *Jugendstil* artists:

Der Dichter [Borchardt] führte mich abends zu einem seiner Freunde, der ein auf dem flachen Dach eines alten Palastes aufgebautes Zimmer bewohnte. Von dem Zimmer aus trat man gleich ins Freie. Unten blinkten die Lichter von Florenz. Wir wurden wie alte Bekannte empfangen. Keiner nannte seinen Namen. Seltsam versonnen wirkte die Persönlichkeit dieses neuen Menschen auf mich. Ich glaubte einen Mönch vor mir zu haben, der seine Hände meist hoch vor den Körper erhob, als wolle er immer ein Gebet beginnen. Dazu kam der weiche, wollige junge Bart, wie ihn Klosterbrüder haben, deren Kinn und Backen nie das Rasiermesser fühlen. Auf dem Rückwege fragte ich meinen Begleiter: "Bei wem sind wir eigentlich gewesen?" "Den müssen Sie doch kennen. Das ist der Dichter Rainer Maria Rilke", war die Antwort.[6]*

Later Vogeler invited Rilke to visit him in Worpswede at the Barkenhoff, the farm house which he had restored and refurbished in the style of *Jugendstil*. Rilke came in December 1898 for a very short stay and then, as mentioned above, in 1900 again.

During his second stay, Rilke totally submerged himself in the atmosphere of this artist colony. He accompanied Clara Westhoff and Paula Becker on their long walks through the countryside while they all discussed their projects and views on art; he visited the studios of Otto Modersohn and Fritz Mackensen among others; and he participated in the regular Sunday evening gatherings at the Barkenhoff where he gladly read from his latest works and joined in the discussions and social activities. He made excursions to Bremen and to Hamburg with the artists, and generally observed how they worked and what their specific techniques were.

In terms of *Jugendstil*, however, it was Heinrich Vogeler who played the most significant role during Rilke's stay in Worpswede. The two artists spent many hours conversing about the tenets of modern art and

---

* "The poet [Borchardt] took me one evening to one of his friends who lived in a room built on the flat roof of an old palace. From the room one stepped directly out into the open. Below, the lights of Florence glistened. We were received as old friends. No one mentioned his name. The personality of this new person appeared curiously pensive to me. I thought that I had a monk before me because he usually held his hands in front of his body as if he were continually wanting to begin a prayer. In addition there was the young, soft, and wooly beard worn as monks wear them whose chins and faces are never touched by a razor. On the way back, I asked my companion: 'At whose house have we been actually?' The answer was: 'You really must know him. That is the poet Rainer Maria Rilke.' "

the goals Vogeler had set for himself in his work, and Rilke had the opportunity for the first time of observing an artist at work in his studio. He records in his diary the following impressions of Vogeler: "Vogeler ist wieder in Adiek. Er hat mir in diesen Tagen so viel erzählt. . . . Er ist überhaupt ein Meister darin, Menschen kurz, durch Farben, Worte oder im Dialoge, zu charakterisieren. Von überall erzählte er: von Brügge und Neapel, von Paris und München, Düsseldorf und Amsterdam. Alles kennt er. Vieles liebt er in der Welt mit einem sehr reichen und nuancierten Gefühl."[7]*

There developed between the two artists a strong bond of admiration and friendship which proved mutually productive for both their artistic careers. As an art critic, Rilke had the opportunity of writing two laudatory and perceptive essays about Vogeler's work, one included in the monograph entitled *Worpswede* and a similar but slightly longer article published in the periodical *Deutsche Kunst und Dekoration*. Rilke also allowed Vogeler to illustrate several of his most important works, including the frontispiece of the first edition of *Das Buch der Bilder* and the collection of poems entitled *Mir zur Feier*. H. W. Petzet writes, furthermore, that it is impossible to consider Vogeler's development as an artist without running again and again across the name of Rainer Maria Rilke.[8] He further speculates that it might have been Rilke who laid the groundwork, through his idealistic and enthusiastic description of Russia, for Vogeler's later decision to emigrate to that country.[9]

Vogeler, for his part, contributed much to Rilke's development, not only as his mentor in artistic techniques but also as a source of inspiration for his poetry. We discover, for example, themes, motifs, and stylistic characteristics similar to Vogeler's throughout Rilke's writing of this period. In addition, Rilke composed many poems based specifically on sketches by Vogeler. In one such series, "Begleitung zu Bildern Heinrich Vogelers" (SW III, 707–11), Rilke portrays the following figures as they appear in Vogeler's sketches: the figure of death arriving in a mysterious boat, a medieval knight at the crossroads of life, and a pale blond maiden just beginning her adult life. In another series (SW III, 699–700), Rilke recreates the themes of the Annunciation and the flight of Mary and Joseph into Egypt just as they had been painted by Vogeler.

The depth of the relationship between Rilke and Vogeler can perhaps best be evaluated in light of an incident which happened some

---

* "Vogeler is in Adiek again. He has told me many things these past few days. . . . He is indeed a master at concisely characterizing people by means of color, words, or dialogue. He spoke of everywhere: Bruges and Naples, Paris and Munich, Dusseldorf and Amsterdam. He knows everything. There is much in the world that he loves with his very deep and sensitive emotions."

years later. In 1912, Vogeler apparently wrote to Rilke and asked to illustrate the poems in *Das Marien-Leben*. Much time had, of course, elapsed since the two artists had worked together, and Rilke's attitudes had changed considerably. Yet he still felt obligated by his earlier friendship, despite misgivings about Vogeler's art, to consider seriously the artist's request. Only after extended correspondence with his publisher and much deliberation did he finally decide that he could not honor the request, but in deference to his old friend, he nevertheless decided to dedicate the collection to him.[10] Vogeler's earlier influence could not, even after so many years, be entirely disregarded.

Rilke left Worpswede in October, 1900, and returned to Berlin. The following spring, he married Clara Westhoff and settled in the neighboring village of Westerwede. Throughout that period, the influence of *Jugendstil* persisted. Even when Rilke went to Paris in the fall of 1902, his thinking and creativity reflected the same orientation. Other forces did begin at that point gradually to impose themselves upon the poet's development, and he never returned exclusively to a *Jugendstil* sphere of influence. Its consequences, however, at least for the works written during this period, were spectacular. In addition to the essays and poems already mentioned, Rilke wrote several more critiques of the various aspects of *Jugendstil*. Between the years 1897 and 1902, he published several poems in *Jugend*, ten poems in *Simplicissimus*, and many poems in *Pan* and *Ver sacrum*. His play, *Die weiße Fürstin*, appeared originally in 1898 in *Pan*, and all of the major works of this period—*Advent, Mir zur Feier, Die Weise von Liebe und Tod des Cornets Christoph Rilke, Geschichten vom lieben Gott, Das Buch der Bilder, Das Stunden-Buch*, and even parts of *Neue Gedichte*—display immense similarity to the art of *Jugendstil*. Many of these works—the early poems, *Die weiße Fürstin, Cornet Rilke*, and *Buch der Bilder*—were revised and reworked during a later period when Rilke already had assumed new ideas that were sometimes foreign to *Jugendstil*. In these revisions, however, the poet consistently retained the original tone and spirit of the work. Even later, then, he did not feel inclined to deny this influence, and indeed its traces can be pursued throughout much of the entire body of his works.

III. Rilke as an Art Critic

Of all the writers of his time, none was more active as a critic than Rilke. Throughout his life, he engaged in the critical evaluation of theater productions, new books, various and sundry artists, and even an occasional concert or ballet performance. He went on lecture tours on which he discussed contemporary poetry or the merits of the works of prominent literary figures such as Detlev von Liliencron or Maurice Maeterlinck. Rilke even got involved from time to time in various social developments, school reform for example, about which he also made his considered opinion known. Some of these essays, reviews, and lectures were produced as a result of Rilke's constant need for additional funds, especially during those difficult Westerwede months. Therefore, these reviews and expressions of opinion were motivated not only by his individual priorities and preferences but also by what he thought would sell well. Others came about as a result only of his sincere desire to contribute to the understanding of a particular event or a particular work. Whatever their motivation, these works verify Rilke's considerable talent and astounding perceptivity as a critic. Because they constitute such a major portion of his writing, they must be viewed by Rilke students with much seriousness.

As has already been stated, Rilke also concerned himself in numerous essays and reviews with the various aspects of *Jugendstil*. These essays have become especially valuable because of their reflection of the poet's own thinking during the period. The two most crucial ventures of this sort, and probably the two most important examples of Rilke's critical writing altogether, are his essays on Heinrich Vogeler and his famous Rodin book. As widely read as they were, these works brought fame both to their subjects and to their author. Today, they provide us with the most valuable insight we have into the poet's relationship with these two artists and with the entire phenomenon of *Jugendstil*.

Although his approach to the works of Vogeler and to those of Rodin is as different as was his relationship with the two artists, Rilke maintained essentially the same perspective in both of these ventures, namely the recording of his own very personalized and subjective reaction to their lives, development, and individual works. With regard to his study of Vogeler, for example, he wrote: "Es wird sich darum handeln, aus dem Gesamt-Inhalt des vorliegenden Werkes und dem

Künstler, der es geschaffen hat, ein Bild zu machen, eine Welt, vor der man schauend stille steht und von der man in bescheidenen Worten spricht" (SW V, 557).* Rilke never made the claim of being objective. He did assert, however, that his personal affinity for these artists and his personal knowledge of their works put him in a far better position to understand them and what they strove to accomplish than other critics. For that reason, he concluded, his views were the only acceptable ones: "Es ist rührend gewesen, was die Verehrer, die ich ihm abgesprochen habe, von Heinrich Vogeler rühmten. . . . Das war sehr rührend, aber auch sehr falsch" (SW V, 561).† That these essays have retained their importance, even today, as works of genuine critical value attests to the intuitive talents on which Rilke openly relied. More important to us, however, is the fact that this personal approach reveals so much about the author himself, what he personally deemed valuable and appropriate, what he personally understood and felt about this art, and by inference, what he perhaps also found useful for his own creativity. It is from this perspective, with a view directed toward the author, that the current discussion will be conducted.

Heinrich Vogeler

During the spring of 1902, while he was still living in the village of Westerwede, Rilke wrote two different essays on the life and works of Heinrich Vogeler. The first and longest of these, entitled simply "Heinrich Vogeler," was written for publication in the well-known *Jugendstil* periodical *Deutsche Kunst und Dekoration* in Darmstadt where it appeared in April of that same year. Rilke's essay was accompanied by twenty-four reproductions of Vogeler's works, nine photographs and seven vignettes and designs. The initial planning for the second essay was begun in January, but the writing itself was not completed until May 1902. It was published along with five other essays about the artists in Worpswede by the Velhagen and Klasing publishing house under the title of *Worpswede*. The writing of these works was motivated by Rilke's desperate need for money, but they demonstrate nonetheless the poet's attraction to his subject and his convictions that what he undertook was

* "The object will be to create a concept of the entire content of the current work and of the artist who created it: a world before which one stands reverently and of which one speaks in modest words."

† "It was touching what his admirers, whom I have denied him, praised in Heinrich Vogeler. . . . It was very touching but also very false."

important. Although apparently written separately and often with a different emphasis on one point or the other, these two essays convey essentially the same ideas. For that reason, we shall consider them together, hoping thereby to get a broader and more complete view of the artist and, of course, the poet.

Because Vogeler, when he was still a relatively young man, was just at the point of becoming known in Germany, Rilke devotes much of his efforts in his essays to Vogeler's background and artistic development. He recounts the artist's studies at the academy in Düsseldorf and his trips to Amsterdam, Italy, and Belgium. After telling of these extensive trips, which were filled with Vogeler's experimentations and imitations of the works of others, Rilke describes how Vogeler decided finally to settle in Worpswede for good. There, Vogeler gave up his tendency toward imitation, having learned in comparison to others what his own talents were and what his own personality required of him, and proceeded now, closed off from the outside world, to realize the promise of his own inner being: "Dieses ist der Sinn und die unausgesprochene Absicht seiner Reisen gewesen; unter dem Einfluß fremder Dinge hat er erkannt, was das Seine ist und wenn etwas an dieser Entwickelung überrascht, so ist es der Umstand, daß er so früh schon sich zu verschließen begann, zu einer Zeit, wo andere junge Leute erst recht aufgehen und sich ziemlich wahllos den Zufällen hingeben, welche ihnen begegnen" (SW V, 119).* In his comments, Rilke reveals several very personal emotional reactions to Vogeler. First, we observe his sympathy with the manner in which Vogeler sought to define the limits and the attributes of his own talent. Rilke himself was engaged in just such a search—in fact his interest in *Jugendstil* art might be considered one phase of it. Second, he displays his admiration and even envy that Vogeler so early in his life had been able to complete his goal of self-realization. Rilke certainly had not. Third, he reveals the basis for his obvious attraction to Vogeler, which is the same foundation upon which Rilke built all of his relationships with artists: his need in times of personal uncertainty and change for a stable, self-confident, and productive mentor from whom he could derive strength. In Worpswede, Vogeler played such a role.

Rilke then turns his attention to that aspect of Vogeler's life to which he felt particularly attracted—the artist's style of life and especially the

* "This was the purpose and the unexpressed intention of his trips; under the influence of foreign things, he recognized what was his own, and if anything is surprising in this development, it is the fact that he began so early to isolate himself at a time when other young people first begin to open themselves up and give themselves over, rather haphazardly, to those chance events which confront them."

3. *Heinrich Vogeler: "Undine" (Worpsweder Archiv, Worpswede)*

physical surroundings in which he lived, his garden and house. Vogeler had bought an old farm house, the Barkenhoff, upon his move to Worpswede and had spent much of his time planting a garden and trees, caring for them, and remodeling and refurnishing the house with furniture and appointments of his own design. Vogeler's garden and house became for Rilke a symbol for a type of earthly paradise into which he believed Vogeler had withdrawn from the distractions of a disturbing world, much the same as a monk might retreat into a monastery to find peace. Within his walled-off paradise, Vogeler created, then, an environment that provided him with the stability and strength of life with which to grow and develop. Here he could hear the "murmuring of his soul": "Da haben wir ein Leben, welches sich mit Mauern umgeben und darauf verzichtet hat, sich über diese Grenzen hinaus auszudehnen. Ein Leben nach Innen. Und dieses Leben verarmt nicht. Inmitten schiffbrüchiger Zeiten scheint es die Zufluchtstätte aller Reichtümer zu sein und wie in einem kleinen zeitlosen Bilde alles zu vereinen, wonach die Tage draußen ringen und jagen" (SW V, 120).* The qualities of self-sufficiency and confidence, and the reverence for and devotion to artistry that this way of life conveyed to Rilke were immensely appealing to him. They especially attracted him since he saw himself still torn and distracted by the superficial and divisive forces of the modern world with no inner reality to which to retreat.

Vogeler's garden and house became for Rilke, in addition, an apt metaphor for the artist's own organic growth in style and technique:

So lebt er sein Leben in den Garten hinein, und dort scheint es sich auf hundert Dinge zu verteilen und auf tausend Arten weiterzuwachsen. In diesen Garten schreibt er seine Gefühle und Stimmungen wie in ein Buch; aber das Buch liegt in den Händen der Natur. . . . So hat er einen Baum gepflanzt oder eine Laube geflochten um des Frühlings willen; und er hat den Baum schlank und zart und die Laube locker gemacht, wie es im Sinne des Frühlings war. Aber die Jahre gehen, der Baum und die Laube verändern sich, sie werden reicher, breiter und schattiger, der ganze Garten wird dichter und rauscht immer mehr. . . . An diesem Garten, an den sich immer steigernden Anforderungen seiner verzweigteren Bäume, ist Heinrich Vogelers Kunst gewachsen; hier waren ihr immer neue, immer schwerere Aufgaben gestellt, Aufgaben, die langsam von Jahr zu Jahr komplizierter wurden und anspruchsvoller (SW V, 125–26).†

* "Here we have a life that has surrounded itself with walls and has declined to extend beyond these limits. A life directed inward. And this life thrives. In the middle of ship-wrecked times, it seems to be the sanctuary of all riches and seems to unite, as in a small timeless image, everything which the days outside struggle for and pursue."

† "Thus he lives his life there in the garden, and there he seems to concentrate on a hundred things and to grow in a thousand ways. In this garden he writes his feelings and

Just as the garden grew and developed and increased in complexity, his works met the challenge of ever more difficult tasks. As the vegetation became more and more lush and strived to fill out the space in the garden with new leaves, limbs, and branches, the organic lines of the artist sought also to fill in the available space in the work, becoming increasingly varied and convoluted: "Seine Liniensprache, welche auf den frühen Radierungen nur wenige Ausdrücke, rhythmisch . . . wiederholte, entnahm dem dichteren Garten tausend Bereicherungen. An Stelle des Lockeren und Lichten, das seinen Blättern und Bildern im Anfang eigentümlich schien, tritt immer mehr das Bestreben, einen gegebenen Raum organisch auszufüllen" (SW V, 126–27).* In this vivid metaphor with which he compares Vogeler's constantly increasing decorative tendencies and his intensified utilization of the *Jugendstil* undulating line to the increasing lushness of the garden, Rilke at once captures two of the primary stylistic characteristics of Vogeler's works and of the works of the *Jugendstil* artists in general. He justifies these characteristics with a type of theoretical basis—the idea of recreating the complexity and the essence of organic nature—which indeed lay in the minds of many of the artists of the day. In addition, he demonstrates his own understanding of some of the more abstract axioms of *Jugendstil* art while revealing his admiration for the movement.

The carefully tended garden provided Vogeler, in Rilke's opinion, with a further artistic opportunity so vital to the art of *Jugendstil* and to Rilke himself. In caring for his garden and in watching it grow and mature, Vogeler came to know and feel the true source of life, that all-pervasive *Lebensstrom* (life's force) which the artists of the period believed was present in all things but invisible and incomprehensible to those living in the over-cultured and superficial society of the time. One of the main goals of the artists of the movement was to rediscover this force and reveal it in their works. Vogeler's garden gave him such insight: "Er weiß in das Leben der kleinsten Blumen hineinzublicken; er kennt sie nicht von Sehen und vom Hörensagen. Er ist in ihr Vertrauen

---

moods as in a book; but the book lies in the hands of nature. . . . Thus he planted a tree or made an arbor because of spring; and he made the tree slender and delicate and the arbor loose as it was meant to be in spring. But the years pass, the tree and the arbor change. They grow more dense, broader, more shady, the entire garden gets thicker and rustles more and more. . . . With the garden and the ever increasing challenges of its bushier trees, Heinrich Vogeler's art grew; here always new and always more difficult tasks were given, tasks which slowly from year to year became more complicated and demanding."

* "His language of lines, which in the earlier etchings repeated only few rhythmical expressions, . . . took from the more lush garden thousands of enrichments. In place of the looser and lighter elements, which seemed in the beginning to be characteristic of his sketches and pictures, the tendency organically to fill out any given area appears."

eingedrungen und wie der Käfer kennt er des Kelches Tiefe und Grund" (SW V, 123–24).* As a result of his reunification with the *Lebensstrom*, Vogeler, in Rilke's view, arrived at a point where he was genuinely in a position to portray this inner and hidden reality in his works:

> Ich habe noch nie eine Wirklichkeit gesehen, die so reich ist und zugleich so tatsächlich und wirklich in jedem Augenblick. Die Wirklichkeit im Leben der Bauern erscheint uns so. . . . Da sind alle Verrichtungen natürlich und notwendig, einfach und gut; und wie aus diesem Leben, ganz von selbst, die Ernten kommen und das Brot, so kommt aus dem Leben Heinrich Vogeler's von selbst eine Kunst, die von seinem Heimats-Lande abhängig ist, die gute und schlechte Jahre hat, die seinen Fleiß, sein Vertrauen und Kraft und Liebe seiner Hände braucht, als ob sie sein Feld wäre und er Säemann und erntender Schnitter dieses Feldes (SW V, 564).†

Rilke then leaves the topic of Vogeler's garden temporarily in order to discuss the other aspect in the artist's life which to that point he felt had exercised an equally profound influence on Vogeler's artistic impulses. This experience was his stay in Munich in 1900 where he served as an illustrator for the *Insel* publications. While there, Vogeler was taken into the elitist circle of artists and writers gathered around Rudolf Alexander Schröder and Alfred Walter Heymel and thus came into contact with many of the important figures of the *Jugendstil* world, including such luminaries as Aubrey Beardsley. These associations opened his eyes to further possibilities in his art and reinforced his own natural predilections:

> Es ist natürlich nicht der reifere Garten allein, der das alles gemacht hat. Die "Insel" ist gegründet worden, die Raum und Anregung bot, die Zeichnungen von Beardsley brachte, welche für Vogeler eine Offenbarung waren und die ihm endlich auch die Bekanntschaft mit Menschen vermittelte, deren große Kultur ihm wohltat und deren Wesen ihn, weil es, gleich dem seinen, auf Verwirklichungen gestimmt war, mit fremdartiger Verwandschaft nahe berührte (SW V, 569).‡

---

* "He knows how to penetrate into the life of the smallest flowers; he doesn't know them only from observing and from having heard about them. He has gained their trust, and like the small insect, he knows the depths and inner foundation of the calyx."

† "I have never yet seen a reality that is so rich and at the same time so factual and real at every moment. The reality in the life of peasants seems like that to us. . . . There, all activities are natural and necessary, simple and good; and just as the harvest and the bread come from this life, of their own accord, from Heinrich Vogeler's life comes an art, of its own accord, which is dependent on his homeland and has good and bad years, needs his diligence, his faith and strength, and the love of his hands as if it were his field and he the sower and the reaper of this field."

‡ "It is, of course, not only the more developed garden that has wrought all this. The

The *Insel* group encouraged Vogeler's earlier interest in the applied arts and taught him how to use glass, cloth, and silver so that the "inner voice" could be heard and the "inner reality" understood. In other words, they intensified Vogeler's search for the *Lebensstrom* and helped him to discover it and reveal it in this instance not in organic form but in the objects he created:

> Im Kreise der "Insel" wuchs er in diese Aufgaben hinein unter jungen Freunden, welche die Stimmen aller Stoffe kannten und die schönen Melodieen, zu denen Silber und Damast und Seide und Glas zusammenklangen, zu komponieren wußten. Dort lernte er die Seele des Silbers verstehen . . . lernte in Silber Dinge dichten, und Lieder schreiben, die das Silber mit seiner glänzenden Stimme sang. . . . Denn die genaue Betrachtung und Kenntnis eines Materials führt zu der Erfahrung, daß keine Stelle daran leer ist und jede anders als die nachbarliche, daß es keine Pausen und Lücken und Verlegenheiten, sondern nur Ausdruck giebt, und daß in diesem Reichtum, in diesem Überfluß der große Zauber schöner Dinge beruht und ihre Bedeutung für das Leben (SW V, 570).*

Upon his return to Worpswede, Vogeler found, according to Rilke, that the new knowledge and experience gained in Munich converged with that which he already possessed from his Worpswede garden, thus providing him with an even stronger harmonious foundation upon which to build his future artistic career.

In the essay *Worpswede*, Rilke then defines one further stylistic aspect of Vogeler's art which, because of its significance in the entire *Jugendstil* movement and because it again indicates Rilke's thorough knowledge of that art, deserves special consideration. This characteristic is Vogeler's unique use of color. Earlier in his works, Rilke observes, Vogeler had used colors in much the same simple, uncomplicated fashion as he had originally used lines. Both had served the single function of lending contour and body to the subject being portrayed and had therefore played an important yet secondary role to the theme:

"Insel" was founded and offered space and stimulation, published sketches by Beardsley —which were a revelation to Vogeler—and provided him [Vogeler] eventually also the acquaintance with people whose great culture was a blessing to him and whose being, because it was directed toward materializations like his, touched him with a strange harmony."

* "He grew into these challenges while under the influence of the "Insel" circle and among young friends who recognized the voices of all materials and knew how to compose the beautiful melodies in which silver, damask, silk, and glass could be harmonized. There he learned to understand the soul of silver . . . learned to write things in silver and to compose songs which were sung by silver with its glittering voice. . . . Because the careful observation and study of a material leads to the understanding that no place in it is empty and each different from its neighbor, that there are no pauses, gaps, or

Die Farbe auf den frühen Bildern Heinrich Vogelers entspricht in gewissem Sinne dem Kontur der ersten Radierungen; sie ist dünn und fließt hell in den Ufern der Umrisse hin. Wie er sich bei dem ersten Wandteppich mit Applikation größerer Seidenstücke bedient, so finden sich auch auf jenen Bildern gleichmäßige, breite Farbenflächen, welche summarisch und gleichsam im Sinne des einfachen Kolorierens gesehen sind (SW V, 130).*

As effective as some of these works were, they did not express the artistic complexity which was to appear later as Vogeler changed and developed his color techniques. In the later works, the colored surfaces, as in the case of the energized lines, no longer had any subordinate function to perform. They acquired a connotative value all of their own and became independent, self-sufficient, and vital elements in the work: "Die Bilder, die nun folgen, sind Versuche, bewegte und lebendige Farben zu malen, Farben, die nichtmehr wie ein Überzug über den Dingen liegen, sondern sich wie fortwährende Ereignisse auf ihrer Oberfläche abspielen" (SW V, 131).†

After having explored Vogeler's life, the major factors in his development, and the overall character of his work, Rilke then turns his attention to several of the individual works. There he discovers all of the attributes which he had earlier recounted. It is clear from these rather lyrical and subjective descriptions just how much the poet identified with the works and saw his own artistic aspirations realized in them. The first to be described is the painting "Mai-Morgen." It is a picture of the Barkenhoff at sunrise, and the house, the trees, the vegetation all seem to come alive as the contours and the colors vibrate in anticipation of the rising sun. In the earlier essay, Rilke writes:

Man betrachte, wie da die Luft gemalt ist, wie die Konturen der Dinge zittern in der frischen frühen Kühle des Sonnen–Aufgangs, wie alles voll Erwachen ist und Atem und Freude. Man glaubt, in dem Rhythmus der Umrisse das Schwingen der vielen Vogel–Stimmen zu fühlen, . . . man glaubt zu sehen, wie die Farben immer mehr Licht empfangen und voller und dunkler werden, und dabei behält man doch das Bewußtsein des Bildes, das Gefühl von einem Bild–Moment, einem Moment der Ruhe, einem Höhepunkt, gleichsam dem

---

embarrassments, only expression, and that in this richness, in this abundance, the great mystery of beautiful things resides along with their meaning for life."

* "The color in Heinrich Vogeler's early pictures corresponds in a certain sense to the contours in the first etchings; it is thin and flows bright within the boundaries of the lines. Just as he appliquéd larger pieces of silk on his first tapestry, one finds in these pictures regular and broad color surfaces that are to be viewed actually as a type of simple coloring."

† "The pictures that now follow are attempts at painting agitated and enlivened colors,

Gipfel des Morgens, von dem es nun abwärts geht in das Tal des Tages (SW V, 571–72).*

In a more specific but still subjective description from the *Worspwede* essay, Rilke evaluates some of the techniques Vogeler used in this work to create the particularly vibrant effects of the light and colors: "Indem er [der Garten] dichter wurde und sich immer mehr anfüllte mit Formen und Farben, veränderte sich auch das Licht, das ihn umgab. Es fiel nichtmehr breit durch das großmaschige Netz zählbarer Äste auf die Wiesen; die Blätter, die Blüten, die Früchte, die Flächen von tausend aneinandergedrängten Dingen fingen es wie kleine Hände auf und spielten damit, glänzten, dunkelten und glühten" (SW V, 131–32).† In both passages, the fundamental qualities of Vogeler's works and of *Jugendstil* are clearly emphasized: the energized lines of the contours, the colors, the emotionally charged atmosphere, and the interplay between color and surface plane.

Two other paintings are subsequently described in the essays. Both of these works, "Melusinen-Märchen" and "Verkündigung," demonstrate the basic types of themes Heinrich Vogeler preferred. Throughout his early creativity he continually returned to the fairy tale, mythology, or biblical stories as subjects for his works and was, as a consequence, generally considered a late romanticist by the general public. In the passages pertaining to these paintings, Rilke emphasizes once more Vogeler's prevalent stylistic traits: the detailed organic forms, profuse decoration, and expertise in the use of color and surfaces. He also underscores the prominence of the emotional aura in the works, which is conveyed not only by the lines and colors but also by the stance and the gesture of the figures. About the "Melusinen-Märchen," he writes:

. . . auch hier ist die Aufgabe, einen Raum organisch auszufüllen, gelöst, diesmal freilich im farbigen Sinne. Wie ein Mosaik in Grün und Gold ist dieser

---

colors that no longer serve only as a covering over things but also as perpetual events which take place on the surface."

* "Notice how the air is painted, how the contours of the things tremble in the early, fresh coolness of the sunrise, how everything is full of awakening, breath, and joy. You think you perceive in the rhythm of the lines the vibrations of the many birds singing, . . . you think you see the colors absorbing more and more light and becoming richer and darker; and at the same time you retain the consciousness of the picture, the impression of a moment in time, a moment of peace, the high point, the peak of the morning from which one proceeds downward into the valley of the day."

† "As it [the garden] got thicker and filled more and more with forms and colors, the light which surrounded it also changed. It no longer fell broadly on the meadows through the large-meshed net of innumerable branches; the leaves, the blossoms, the fruit, the surfaces of a thousand things joined together captured it like small hands and played with it, glistened, grew dark, and glowed."

wildernde Wald gesehen, aus dessen flimmernder Tiefe das staunende Mädchengesicht dem tumben Eisenmann entgegensieht, der heiß und hilflos in der Rüstung steht. . . . Es ist vielleicht das Unvergeßlichste in dem Bilde, wie das Melusinenmädchen mit dieser Wirrnis übervielen Dingen verflochten ist, so daß man nicht sagen kann, wo es beginnt, und ob es nicht die bangen Augen des Waldes selber sind, die sich, neugierig und beunruhigt zugleich, auftun vor dem Unbekannten (SW V, 132).*

In his discussion of "Verkündigung," Rilke particularly emphasizes the emotional aura. Here it is created by the position of the two figures relative to one another, by their facial expression, and by the luxurious lines of the angel's robes: "Der Engel, der die Botschaft bringt, erschreckt sie nicht. Er ist der Gast, den sie erwartet hat, und sie ist seinen Worten eine weitoffene Flügeltür und ein schöner Empfang. Und der große Engel steht über sie geneigt und singt so nah, daß sie keines seiner Worte verlieren kann, und in den Falten seines reichen Kleides steht die Bewegung noch, mit der er sich zu ihr niederließ" (SW V, 133).†

As his final point in the essays, Rilke gives his own interpretation of Vogeler's use of the fairy tale, mythological, or biblical themes and their significance. Severely misunderstood by the general public in Rilke's opinion, these themes had little to do with their original sources and certainly were not designed to effect a revival of the romantic age. Rather, they became the vehicle for Vogeler to portray symbolically the qualities of his all-important, isolated "garden" world:

Man hat sie [die Märchen] lange für die Träume eines späten Romantikers gehalten. . . . Aber weder die "Schlangen-Braut", noch das "Frosch-KönigsMärchen" sind aus vorhandenen Märchen-Stoffen heraus entstanden, und die "Sieben Raben" sind nur eine Maske, hinter der sieben schwarze Vögel ungestört ihr Wesen treiben dürfen. . . . Das war kein naiver Romantiker, der diese Blätter schuf, die er lange nach ihrer Vollendung mit dem zunächstliegenden Märchen-Namen verkleidete, das war ein Mensch unserer Zeit. . . . Ein Mensch mit einer schon ganz bestimmten, aber sehr eng begrenzten Wirklichkeit um

---

* ". . . here too the challenge of organically filling out a space is met, this time, to be sure, in the sense of colors. This forest wilderness is seen as a mosaic of green and gold from the glimmering depths of which the surprised face of the maiden looks toward the simple iron man who stands hot and helpless in his armour. . . . Perhaps the most unforgettable thing about the picture is how the figure of the Melusina-maiden is woven into this confused myriad of things so that one cannot say where she begins or if it perhaps isn't the anxious eyes of the forest itself that, curious and at the same time disquieted, open up in front of the stranger."

† "The angel who brings the message does not startle her. He is the guest whom she has expected, and she is a 'wide open door' for his words and a lovely welcome. And the great angel stands bending over her and sings so closely that she misses none of his words and in the folds of his rich cloak are still the movements with which he came down to her."

sich, zu der alles in Widerspruch stand, was er als Erlebnis oder Stimmung empfing. . . . So entstanden diese Märchen, seine eigenen Märchen, Erlebnisse, die über seine Wirklichkeit hinausragten, und die er mit den wenigen Mitteln dieser Wirklichkeit auszusprechen sich bemühte (SW V, 560–61).*

In another passage, Rilke writes: "Die Anregung zu der Radierung von den sieben Schwänen kam nicht von dem Märchen her, und die Entwürfe dieses schönen Marienlebens sind nicht über dem Lesen der Bibel gereift. Es war wieder die Wirklichkeit, die sich diese Bilder schuf, und der Garten Heinrich Vogeler's, in dem sie sich irgendwo ereigneten" (SW V, 574).† Rilke touches here upon one of the main characteristics not only of Vogeler's thinking but of the thinking of *Jugendstil* artists in general. Just like Vogeler, most of these artists sought to withdraw from their unsympathetic contemporary surroundings, and they usually portrayed this retreat thematically in some form in their works. Vogeler, as Rilke explains above, had retreated in real life into his garden paradise; in his works, his retreat was represented by the subjective world of the fairy tale and by personal variations on Biblical or mythological figures.

In his essays on Vogeler, Rilke created a vivid picture of the artist's development and a description of the fundamental qualities which form the basis of his works. He emphasized throughout his essays those qualities which are peculiar to Vogeler but also intrinsic to the entire *Jugendstil* movement. Furthermore, it becomes increasingly apparent that Rilke, through his subjective approach, really arrived at his judgements by means of a strong personal affinity for the artist's work and for the movement at large.

Auguste Rodin

Rilke first became aware of Rodin and his work through conversations he had with Paula Becker and Clara Westhoff while still in Worps-

* "The fairy tales were considered for a long time as the dreams of a late romanticist. . . . But neither the "Snake Bride" nor the "Frog King" arose from the fairy tale material, and the "Seven Ravens" are only a mask behind which seven black birds can live out their natural inclinations undisturbed. . . . The one who created these sketches, to which he gave the handiest title long after they were completed, was no naive romanticist. He was a man of our time. . . . A person living in an entirely defined but very narrowly limited reality to which all of his experiences and impressions stood in conflict. . . . This is the origin of his fairy tales, his own fairy tales, experiences which were projected beyond his reality and which he attempted to express with the limited means of that reality."

† "The stimulation for the etching of the seven swans did not come from the fairy tale, and the sketches of this beautiful life of Mary did not mature from reading the Bible. It was

wede, and he was most impressed by their opinion.[1] Although his interest in Rodin continued, it was not until the spring of 1902, after the successful completion of the Vogeler essays and again primarily as a result of severe financial distress, that he decided to undertake a critical investigation of the sculptor's works. He consequently began negotiations with Richard Muther for the writing of a monograph which he hoped to have included in a series of monographs on various artists to be published by the Julius Bard press in Berlin. Upon the completion of these negotiations early in the summer of 1902, the poet wrote Rodin, apparently received encouragement, and began his background investigation. In September of that year, armed with his considerable experience in critical writing and his continuing enthusiasm for the art of *Jugendstil*, Rilke arrived in Paris prepared to initiate the actual study. A few days later, he met Rodin for the first time. Although Rodin spoke no German and Rilke's French was less than adequate, a cordial relationship between them ensued which included among other things a series of conversations about art and sculpture and the personal philosophy of the master. Though overwhelmed, Rilke felt an immediate and profound affinity for Rodin and set out with astonishing zeal and dedication to commit his observations and ideas about the sculptor to paper. By Christmas, his work was finished and by the following spring, the monograph had already appeared.[2]

The book's evaluation of Rodin's works was revolutionary for its time and is surprisingly valid even in our day. More than half a century later, it has retained its position of respect among art historians and appears in all of the major Rodin bibliographies. Albert Elsen writes, for example:

The memorable sentences of the poet, R. M. Rilke, who served for a time as Rodin's secretary and remained one of his most loyal friends and admirers, stands apart with lithic durability from the glutinous sentimentality and inflated chauvinism that characterizes much of the literature of the sculptor and his art. In Rilke's penetrating essay . . . one finds many statements unsurpassed in the depth and lucidity of their insight.[3]

When the book was first published in English, the editors for *The Connoisseur* wrote:

Slight as this book is, it is rich in content. . . . Besides being a fervent disciple, [Rilke] is a poet of real sensibility, and further, his book has the merit of obvious sincerity. . . . Unlike so much fashionable criticism of to-day, it is full of under-

---

again reality which created these pictures and the garden of Heinrich Vogeler in which somewhere they took place."

standing and sane observations finely expressed. . . . He has looked intelligently as well as admiringly at Rodin's works and is able to interpret to others the mastery he finds in them.[4]

Rilke scholars also have studied the Rodin book with great interest.[5] To them it is a clear indication of the profound effect Rodin was to have upon the future of the poet in his attempts at gaining control over his creative impulses, for example, and in his struggle to surmount the subjective self. These critics have failed, however, to consider the book in relation to Rilke's past and to the persistent influence that *Jugendstil* exercised on him. It is, however, this movement which formed the real basis for Rilke's analysis of Rodin's works and the true perspective from which his monograph was written. It becomes evident upon careful scrutiny of the book that Rilke, without ever saying so explicitly, considered Rodin's works in many respects as a continuation of the *Jugendstil* tradition.

Based on this fact, the Rodin book assumes special importance in our current study. Not only must Rodin be considered in a new light, since, with the exception of his early works, he is not generally viewed as a representative of the European *Art Nouveau*; but, more significantly, Rilke's own activities in Paris at the time he wrote the book take on new and unexpected ramifications. No longer can Rilke's period in the French capital be thought of exclusively as the startling beginning of a new period in the poet's life in which he completely suppressed the past and courageously confronted the future. The Rodin book testifies from beginning to end to the lingering influence of the past and also to the fact that the transition between his earlier and his middle periods of creativity was only a very gradual one. The *Jugendstil* movement continued to color Rilke's life even in Paris despite (or perhaps because of) the harsh realities of the big city and modern life.

The poet approached the Rodin book in much the same fashion as he had written about Vogeler. He sought no scholarly objectivity nor did he claim to be an impartial observer. Rather, he openly admitted to a bias toward Rodin, and, as with Vogeler, he believed that this personal approach enabled him all the more to penetrate to the essence of the works and arrive at a more valid and truthful statement than might otherwise have been possible. The language of the book is as lyrical as that of the Vogeler essays, and Rilke once more sought not only to provide an external description of the works but to capture their inner reality as well.

In the initial section of his monograph, Rilke recognizes in Rodin several major characteristics that he had also seen in Vogeler and that he knew to be fundamental to the *Jugendstil* movement. Rodin too, in

Rilke's opinion, had isolated himself from a hostile world and, alone with his soul and oblivious of the non-artistic and divisive forces outside his protected enclave, had determined his own development and future. As a result of his personal isolation, his works assumed the same ambience of self-sufficiency and separation from outer surroundings that Vogeler's had demonstrated: "Was die Dinge auszeichnet, dieses Ganz–mit–sich–Beschäftigtsein, das war es, was einer Plastik ihre Ruhe gab; sie durfte nichts von außen verlangen oder erwarten, sich auf nichts beziehen, was draußen lag, nichts sehen, was nicht in ihr war. Ihre Umgebung mußte *in* ihr liegen" (SW V, 159).* As early as the fall of 1900, shortly after Rilke first became interested in Rodin, he had written:

RODIN: Das macht seine Plastik so isoliert, so sehr zum Kunstwerk, welches wie eine Festung ist: sich selbst beschützend, wehrhaft, unzugänglich, nur solchen, die Flügel fühlen, durch ein Wunder erreichbar: daß sie meistens sich befreit hat von der Abhängigkeit von Umgebung und Hintergrund, vor ihrem eigenen Stein, wie zögernd, stehen geblieben ist, auf den Lippen des Gebirges, das angefangen hat zu erzählen (SW V, 249).†

It is obvious that Rilke's views did not change when he personally met the artist and when he observed his works firsthand.

In his art, Rodin too, according to Rilke, had sought to rediscover the underlying and unifying *Lebensstrom*, so vital a part of *Jugendstil* theory. This search the sculptor undertook with his repeated artistic experimentations during which he struggled to eliminate the superficial, artificial, and lifeless elements from his works while at the same time attempting to rediscover the essence of life. Only after years of toil was he successful in this task. Now in his works, particularly in his portrayal of the human body, Rilke observed an unmistakable expression of the primordial power. In Rilke's view, this quality formed one of Rodin's predominant characteristics. He writes: "Wenn man ihn [den menschlichen Körper] jetzt aufdeckte, vielleicht enthielt er tausend Ausdrücke für alles Namenlose und Neue, das inzwischen entstanden war, und für jene alten Geheimnisse, die, aufgestiegen aus dem Unbewußten, wie fremde Flußgötter ihre triefenden Gesichter aus dem Rauschen des

---

* "That which distinguished the objects, that element of being entirely caught up in itself, is what gave his sculpture its quietude; it was not permitted to look for or expect anything from outside itself, to establish a relationship with anything that lay outside, to see anything that was not in itself. Its surroundings had to be *within* itself."

† "RODIN: That is what makes his sculpture so isolated, so very much a work of art that is like a fortress, defending itself, combative, impregnable, only reachable through a miracle by those who perceive wings—it has usually freed itself from a dependence on its surroundings and backdrop, and has, as if hesitating, remained standing before its own stone on the brink of the mountain that has begun to speak."

Blutes hoben" (SW V, 146–47).* The references to the "old mysteries" which rise "from the subconscious like strange river gods from the pulsations of the blood" are so typical of phrases used by Rilke in his own poetry to portray the forces of the *Lebensstrom* that it is clear just what he was attempting to describe in Rodin's work. Particularly in the preliminary studies for Rodin's momentous "Gates of Hell," Rilke discerns a rediscovery of this primordial power: "Er [Rodin] fand die Gebärden der Urgötter, die Schönheit und Geschmeidigkeit der Tiere, den Taumel alter Tänze und die Bewegungen vergessener Gottesdienste seltsam verbunden mit den neuen Gebärden, die entstanden waren in der langen Zeit, während welcher die Kunst abgewendet war und allen diesen Offenbarungen blind" (SW V, 170).† Here it is the gestures of the primeval gods, the beauty of the animals, and the ecstasy and frenzy of the primitive worship which reveal the forgotten "life's force." The more "civilized" and superficial gestures of the recent past, which are also present in these studies, stand in stark contrast to the more "vital" ones. The ones of the recent past are confused, disordered, and meaningless:

Diese neuen Gebärden . . . waren ungeduldig. Wie einer, der lange nach einem Gegenstand sucht, immer ratloser wird, zerstreuter und eiliger, und um sich herum eine Zerstörung schafft, eine Anhäufung von Dingen, die er aus ihrer Ordnung zieht, als wollte er sie zwingen mitzusuchen, so sind die Gebärden der Menschheit, die ihren Sinn night finden kann, ungeduldiger geworden, nervöser, rascher und hastiger (SW V, 170).‡

Rilke discovers other major *Jugendstil* characteristics throughout Rodin's works as well. One of these is the typical dichotomy between vitalism and resignation or between asceticism and bacchanalianism. This feature he finds particularly evident in the work "Everlasting Idol":

* "If it [the human body] were now revealed, perhaps it would contain a thousand expressions of everything that is nameless and new that has come into being in the meantime, of these old mysteries which, having risen from the subconscious, raise their dripping faces like strange river gods from the pulsations of the blood."

† "He [Rodin] discovered that the gestures of the primeval gods, the beauty and suppleness of animals, the ecstasy of old dances, and the movement of forgotten worship ceremonies are strangely related to the new gestures which arose during the prolonged period in which art had turned away and was blind to all of these revelations."

‡ "These new gestures . . . were impatient. Like someone who has been looking for something for a long time and becomes more and more frustrated, confused and harried, who creates great disorder around himself, a great pile of things which he has taken from their ordered places as if he wanted to force them to search with him—just so, the gestures of humanity, that cannot find its purpose, have become more and more impatient, nervous, impetuous, and hurried."

Und man glaubt plötzlich in der Haltung, in die dieses junge Mädchen aus Trägheit, aus Träumerei oder aus Einsamkeit verfiel, eine uralte heilige Gebärde zu erkennen, in welche die Göttin ferner, grausamer Kulte versunken war. Der Kopf dieses Weibes neigt sich ein wenig vor; mit einem Ausdruck von Nachsicht, Hoheit und Geduld, sieht sie, wie aus der Höhe einer stillen Nacht, auf den Mann hinab, der sein Gesicht in ihre Brust versenkt wie in viele Blüten. . . . Etwas von der Stimmung eines Purgatorio lebt in diesem Werke. Ein Himmel ist nah, aber er ist noch nicht erreicht; eine Hölle ist nah, aber sie ist noch nicht vergessen. Auch hier strahlt aller Glanz von der Berührung aus; von der Berührung der beiden Körper und von der Berührung des Weibes mit sich selbst (SW V, 166–67).*

Combined in the figure of this woman are a certain pensiveness, reserve, and loneliness on the one hand and the surging passion of primeval emotion on the other. Both "heaven" and "hell" find expression. The "Gates of Hell" incorporate the same extremes: "Hier waren die Laster und die Lästerungen, die Verdammnisse und die Seligkeiten, und man begriff auf einmal, daß eine Welt arm sein mußte, die das alles verbarg und vergrub und tat, als ob es nicht wäre. Es war" (SW V, 169).†

A second characteristic is the typical "sanctified" air of the *Jugendstil* work. Rodin's sculptures, according to Rilke, often assume the qualities of altar pieces, and the initiated observer is compelled by their power to display a worshipful reverence and devotion before them: "Und doch mußte es sich irgendwie von den anderen Dingen unterscheiden, den gewöhnlichen Dingen, denen jeder ins Gesicht greifen konnte. Es mußte irgendwie unantastbar werden, sakrosankt, getrennt vom Zufall und von der Zeit, in der es einsam und wunderbar wie das Gesicht eines Hellsehers aufstand" (SW V, 149).‡

---

* "And suddenly we believe we recognize in the posture which this young maiden—because of inertia, dreaminess, or loneliness—has assumed, a primeval, sacred gesture in which the goddess of distant, gruesome cults was caught up. The head of this woman inclines forward a bit; with an expression of indulgence, haughtiness ,and patience, she looks down as from the heights of a quiet night on the man who sinks his face into her bosom as into many blossoms. . . . Something of the atmosphere of purgatory exists in this work. Heaven is near, but not yet reached; hell is near, but not yet forgotten. Here too, all lustre radiates from the touch, from the contact of the two bodies, and from the woman's touch of herself."

† "Here were the depravities and the blasphemies, the perditions and the bliss, and one realized suddenly that a world would be deprived where all of this was hidden and buried and where it was pretended that it did not exist. It did."

‡ "And yet it had somehow to distinguish itself from other things, the common things which everyone comprehends. It had somehow to become untouchable, sacrosanct, separated from coincidence and from the era in which it arose alone and wonderful like the face of a clairvoyant."

After the initial section of the monograph, Rilke proceeds to a rather detailed discussion of most of Rodin's major works: "The Man with the Broken Nose," "The Age of Bronze," "Balzac," "The Citizens of Calais," "John the Baptist," "The Kiss," "Victor Hugo," and, of course, "The Gates of Hell." In all of these, he emphasizes typical *Jugendstil* qualities which reveal his own artistic bias. In particular, his investigation of the various structural elements in each work points to the poet's orientation and preference for the art of *Jugendstil*. This is true of his attention to Rodin's use of the *Fläche* (surface plane), for example. As most major critics of *Jugendstil* have recognized, the *Fläche* played an especially prominent role in the art of that period. It was the basic stylistic element of the art work and through it such typical characteristics as the pronounced silhouette and the vitality of movement were in part created.[6] Other critics, Wolfdietrich Rasch for example,[7] have seen in the use of the *Fläche* an artistic attempt at reducing the subject to its basic element in order then to recreate it into a new unity which more fully reflected the true reality of the universe.

Although Rilke described sculpture in his monograph and not painting and was not concerned with the destruction of dimension and volume as such, he nevertheless ascribed to the *Fläche*, as the basic structural element in Rodin's works, the same artistic function as that in the works described by Rasch and others. In depicting the sculptor's early development, Rilke writes:

In diesem Augenblick hatte Rodin das Grundelement seiner Kunst entdeckt, gleichsam die Zelle seiner Welt. Das war die Fläche, diese verschieden große, verschieden betonte, genau bestimmte Fläche, aus der alles gemacht werden mußte. . . . Mit dieser Entdeckung begann Rodins eigenste Arbeit. Nun erst waren alle herkömmlichen Begriffe der Plastik für ihn wertlos geworden. Es gab weder Pose, noch Gruppe, noch Komposition. Es gab nur unzählbar viele lebendige Flächen, es gab nur Leben, und das Ausdrucksmittel, das er sich gefunden hatte, ging gerade auf dieses Leben zu (SW V, 150).*

In Rilke's view, then, Rodin, like the *Jugendstil* artists before him, disregarded traditional concepts of art and constructed his universe from individual *Flächen*. This technique, as in a typical *Jugendstil* work, resulted in a unique and vital reality in which all elements are united into

---

* "In this moment, Rodin discovered the basic element of his art and at the same time the cell of his world. It was the surface plane, this varyingly large, varyingly emphasized, exactly determined surface plane from which everything had to be made. . . . With this discovery, Rodin's real work began. Now finally, all inherited concepts of sculpture became useless to him. There was neither pose, nor grouping, nor composition. There were only myriads of living surfaces, there was only life, and the means of expression which he had discovered for himself went right to the heart of this life."

one whole. The emotional impact of Rodin's "Man with the Broken Nose," according to Rilke, stems primarily from the unity of these individual, living surfaces: "Aber nicht aus der unvergleichlichen Durchbildung allein ergiebt sich diese Schönheit. Sie entsteht aus der Empfindung des Gleichgewichts, des Ausgleichs aller dieser bewegten Flächen untereinander, aus der Erkenntnis dessen, daß alle diese Erregungsmomente in dem Dinge selbst ausschwingen und zu Ende gehen" (SW V, 157).* In Rodin's "Age of Bronze," the *Flächen* also serve to reveal the vital "life's force"; each surface forms an expressive unity by itself, and together they create a figure of awesome unity and power: "Das strengste Auge konnte an dieser Figur keinen Platz entdecken, der weniger lebendig, weniger bestimmt und klar gewesen wäre. Es war, als stiege in die Adern dieses Mannes Kraft aus den Tiefen der Erde" (SW V, 160).†

A second structural element to be found in all of Rodin's works is what Tschudi Madsen calls "the cult of line"—the "asymmetrically undulating line terminating in a whiplike, energy-laden movement."[8] Because of this line, *Jugendstil* work is inherently energetic and rhythmical. Furthermore, the dynamic lines supplement the surface planes as the basic compositional element. They permeate the figures themselves and their surroundings and unify the various elements of the work while displaying the vital and powerful forces of life, the portrayal of which, as we have seen, formed one of the major goals of *Jugendstil*.

Rilke never diminished the importance of the *Fläche* as the basic structural element of Rodin's sculpture, for he believed these surfaces to be so charged with energy that they, in a sense, emanated electronic waves, like those actually portrayed in a *Jugendstil* work. They inspirited each work, causing it to come to life and uniting it with its surroundings. In other words, the dynamic lines Rilke perceived were purely emotional ones, yet, in their effect, they possessed the same qualities as any other *Jugendstil* work.

In Rodin's "The Kiss," Rilke finds emotional waves pervading both of the figures and bestowing them with beauty and power:

Der Zauber der großen Gruppe des Mädchens und des Mannes, die *Der Kuß* genannt wird, liegt in dieser weisen und gerechten Verteilung des Lebens; man

---

* "But this beauty is not only a result of the incomparable composition. It arises from the impression of balance, from the equalization of all of these animated surface planes, from the knowledge that all of these moments of agitation reverberate and come to an end within the limits of the object itself."

† "The most critical eye could not discover in this figure a place which was less alive, less defined and clear. It was as if power rose up from the depths of the earth into the veins of this man."

hat das Gefühl, als gingen hier von allen Berührungsflächen Wellen in die Körper hinein, Schauer von Schönheit, Ahnung und Kraft. Daher kommt es, daß man die Seligkeit dieses Kusses überall auf diesen Leibern zu schauen glaubt; er ist wie eine Sonne, die aufgeht, und sein Licht liegt überall (SW V, 165).*

In other works Rilke sees these waves reverberating from the statue into the surrounding space, filling it with the contours of the figures. In such a manner, not unlike Peter Behren's "Kiss," the figures and the entire surroundings are unified, and the space itself becomes part of the art work. Rilke says:

Wenn Rodin das Bestreben hatte, die Luft so nahe als möglich an die Oberfläche seiner Dinge heranzuziehen, so ist es, als hätte er hier den Stein geradezu in ihr aufgelöst: Der Marmor scheint nur der feste fruchtbare Kern zu sein und sein letzter leisester Kontur schwingende Luft. Das Licht, welches zu diesem Steine kommt, verliert seinen Willen; es geht nicht über ihn hin zu anderen Dingen; es schmiegt sich ihm an, es zögert, es verweilt, es wohnt in ihm (SW V, 198–99).†

In the case of a group of figures such as the "Citizens of Calais," the wave-filled air serves as the unifying force not only of the statues and the space surrounding them but also of the individual figures themselves. The viewer therefore perceives only one figure and one work, not a constellation or grouping of statues. About the "Citizens of Calais," Rilke says:

Hätte man den Versuch gemacht, man hätte eine unvergleichliche Gelegenheit gehabt, die Geschlossenheit dieser Gruppe zu bewundern, die aus sechs Einzelfiguren bestand und doch so fest zusammenhielt, als wäre sie nur ein einziges Ding. Und dabei berührten die einzelnen Gestalten einander nicht, sie standen nebeneinander wie die letzten Bäume eines gefällten Waldes, und was sie vereinte, war nur die Luft, die an ihnen teilnahm in einer besonderen Art. Ging man um diese Gruppe herum, so war man überrascht zu sehen, wie aus dem Wellenschlag der Konturen rein und groß die Gebärden stiegen, sich erhoben, standen und zurückfielen in die Masse, wie Fahnen, die man einzieht. Da war alles klar und bestimmt (SW V, 192–93).‡

---

* "The fascination of the wonderful statue of the maiden and the man, which is called 'The Kiss,' lies in the wise and equitable distribution of life; one has the feeling here that from all contact points waves pulsate into the bodies, shudders of beauty, anticipation, and power. For that reason, one believes he sees the bliss of that kiss everywhere on these bodies; it is like the sun which rises, and its light shines everywhere."

† "If Rodin had the goal in mind of drawing the air as near as possible to the surface of his objects, it is here as if he had almost dissolved the stone in it. The marble appears to be only the solid, fruitful center whose last and softest contour is the vibrating air. The light which shines on this stone surrenders its will and does not go beyond it to other objects. It nestles against the stone, it hesitates, it tarries, it resides in it."

‡ "If one had made the attempt, one would have had a splendid opportunity to admire the

Two other structural elements of Rodin's works, though not as basic to *Jugendstil* as the *Fläche* and the line, also occupy Rilke's attention throughout his discussion of the various works. If in a *Jugendstil* work the view of the world seems incomplete or distorted, if the frame of a picture dissects the arm of the main figure, or if the branches of the tree grow beyond the painting into the frame or even onto the wall, it is, once again, because the artist has attempted to find and depict a reality that transcends the limits of his work. A detailed, well-proportioned, "realistic" portrayal or a "well-made" work of art is unimportant to him. Rasch says that the typical *Jugendstil* work represents: ". . . ein Ausschnitt aus dem unendlichen Fließen der Dinge und Gestalten, das jenseits der Bildränder weitergeht. . . . Das Bild zeigt einen Teil des unendlichen Gewebes, in dem jedes mit jedem verflochten ist und das einzelne wenig, der Zusammenhang alles bedeutet. An welcher Stelle der Bildausschnitt den Zusammenhang unterbricht, ist gleichgültig, da nur der Zusammenhang, nicht das einzelne Gebilde zählt."[9]*

Rilke recognized this same *Jugendstil* "arbitrariness" in Rodin's works. He felt compelled in his book to defend the sculptor against his many critics who thought that Rodin's statues were poorly composed, often left incomplete (i.e., the Balzac statue), and lacked much in the way of artistic polish. Rilke believed, as did the *Jugendstil* artists, that such works often revealed more of the true reality of the world than more traditional art. In a passage concerning the statue "Interior Voice," he indicates surprise that in relation to sculpture some of Rodin's critics, who had by now learned to accept such features in painting, still held fast to antiquated concepts of art from the past:

Es ist nicht lange her, da lehnte man sich in derselben Weise gegen die vom Bildrande abgeschnittenen Bäume der Impressionisten auf; man hat sich sehr rasch an diesen Eindruck gewöhnt, man hat, für den Maler wenigstens, einsehen und glauben gelernt, daß ein künstlerisches Ganzes nicht notwendig mit dem gewöhnlichen Ding-Ganzen zusammenfallen muß, daß, unabhängig da-

---

unity of this grouping which consisted of six individual figures and yet was so solidly held together that it seemed to be one single object. But the individual figures did not even touch each other, they stood beside one another like the last trees of a forest that has been felled, and only the air united them and was united with them in a special way. If one went around this grouping, one was surprised to see how the gestures, pure and majestic, rose from the waves of the contours, stood, and fell back into the mass as if they were flags being drawn in. All of this was clear and certain."

* ". . . a portion of the infinte flowing of things and figures which goes beyond the picture itself. . . . The picture shows only a section of the infinite tapestry in which everything is united with everything else, the individual thing meaning little, the cohesive unity everything. It is immaterial at what point the picture interrupts this overall unity since only this continuity and not the individual picture counts."

von, innerhalb des Bildes neue Einheiten entstehen, neue Zusammenschlüsse, Verhältnisse und Gleichgewichte (SW V, 163).*

In describing Rodin's many studies of the human hand, Rilke views them as complete and totally realistic works which are capable of expressing any human emotion:

Dem Künstler steht es zu, aus vielen Dingen eines zu machen und aus dem kleinsten Teil eines Dinges eine Welt. Es giebt im Werke Rodins Hände, selbständige, kleine Hände, die, ohne zu irgend einem Körper zu gehören, lebendig sind. Hände, die sich aufrichten, gereizt und böse, Hände, deren fünf gesträubte Finger zu bellen scheinen wie die fünf Hälse eines Höllenhundes. Hände, die gehen, schlafende Hände, und Hände, welche erwachen; verbrecherische, erblich belastete Hände . . . (SW V, 163–64).†

Rilke also discovered in Rodin's works the *Jugendstil* predilection for the meaningful gesture or stance through which the artist casts a particular aura around his figures or creates a particular mood. These emotional qualities often signify the underlying meaning of the work and as such play a vital role in its structure. In describing Rodin's "Age of Bronze" (illus. 4), he says:

Diese Gestalt ist auch noch in anderem Sinne bedeutsam. Sie bezeichnet im Werke Rodins die Geburt der Gebärde. Jene Gebärde, die wuchs und sich allmählich zu solcher Größe und Gewalt entwickelte, hier entsprang sie wie eine Quelle, welche leise an diesem Leibe niederrann. Sie erwachte im Dunkel der ersten Zeiten und sie scheint, in ihrem Wachsen, durch die Weite dieses Werkes wie durch alle Jahrtausende zu gehen, weit über uns hinaus zu denen, die kommen werden. Zögernd entfaltet sie sich in den erhobenen Armen; und diese Arme sind noch so schwer, daß die Hand des einen schon wieder ausruht auf der Höhe des Hauptes. Aber sie schläft nichtmehr, sie sammelt sich; ganz hoch oben auf dem Gipfel des Gehirnes, wo es einsam ist, bereitet sie sich vor auf die Arbeit, auf die Arbeit der Jahrhunderte, die nicht Absehn noch Ende hat. Und in dem rechten Fuße steht wartend ein erster Schritt (SW V, 160–61).‡

* "It has not been long since people rejected in the same fashion the trees of the Impressionists which were cut off by the frame of the picture. But they very quickly got used to this effect and acquired, at least with regard to painters, an understanding and a belief that an artistic whole need not correspond to the ordinary whole of objects, that, completely independently, new unities arise within the picture, new affinities, relationships, and equilibria."

† "It is incumbent upon the artist to create a unity out of many objects and from the smallest particle of an object a world. There are in Rodin's works hands, independent, small hands, that, without being attached to any body, are alive. Hands which arise, irritated and angry, hands whose five bristling fingers appear to bark like the five necks of a dog of hell. Hands that walk, sleeping hands, and hands that awaken; villainous, congenitally afflicted hands."

‡ "This figure is meaningful in still another way. It illustrates in Rodin's works the birth of the gesture. That gesture, which grew and developed gradually to such majesty and

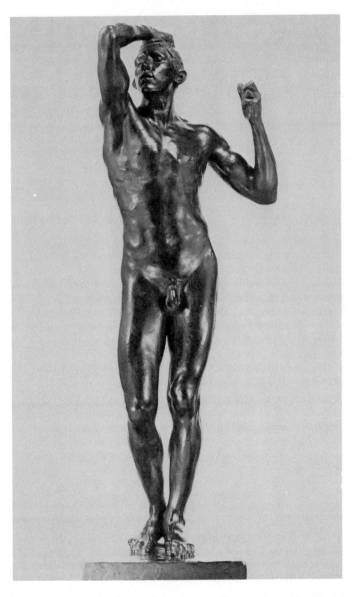

4. *Auguste Rodin: "The Age of Bronze" (Musée Rodin, Paris)*

In Rilke's description, the gesture and the stance of the figure become more significant than the figure itself. In the gesture alone, man's past (and for that matter, the past of all of mankind) and his future come to life. The mood of the work, its true reality, transcends the actual work itself.

In another section of his analysis of "Interior Voice" (a passage which because of its unmistakably *Jugendstil* ambience we shall quote in its entirety), Rilke continues his evaluation of Rodin's use of the gesture in endowing his figures with a greater reality and context. In this instance it is the torso of the statue which expresses that "distant pulsation of life":

Niemals ist ein menschlicher Körper so um sein Inneres versammelt gewesen, so gebogen von seiner eigenen Seele und wieder zurückgehalten von seines Blutes elastischer Kraft. Und wie auf dem tief seitwärts gesenkten Leibe der Hals sich ein wenig aufrichtet und streckt und den horchenden Kopf über das ferne Rauschen des Lebens hält, das ist so eindringlich und groß empfunden, daß man sich keiner ergreifenderen und verinnerlichteren Gebärde zu erinnern weiß. Es fällt auf, daß die Arme fehlen. Rodin empfand sie in diesem Fall als eine zu leichte Lösung seiner Aufgabe, als etwas, was nicht zu dem Körper gehört, der sich in sich selber hüllen wollte, ohne fremde Hülfe. Man kann an die Duse denken, wie sie in einem Drama d'Annunzio's, schmerzhaft verlassen, ohne Arme zu umarmen versucht und zu halten ohne Hände. Diese Szene, in der ihr Körper eine Liebkosung lernte, die weit über ihn hinausging, gehört zu den Unvergeßlichkeiten ihres Spieles. Es vermittelte den Eindruck, daß die Arme ein Überfluß waren, ein Schmuck, eine Sache der Reichen und der Unmäßigen, die man von sich werfen konnte, um ganz arm zu sein. Nicht also hätte sie Wichtiges eingebüßt, wirkte sie in diesem Augenblick; eher wie einer, der seinen Becher verschenkt, um aus dem Bache zu trinken, wie ein Mensch, der nackt ist und noch ein wenig hülflos in seiner tiefen Blöße. So ist es auch bei den armlosen Bildsäulen Rodins; es fehlt nichts Notwendiges. Man steht vor ihnen als vor etwas Ganzem, Vollendetem, das keine Ergänzung zuläßt (SW V, 162–63).*

---

power, arose here like a spring which softly ran down this body. It awoke in the darkness of primordial times, and it appears, in its growth, to proceed through the vastness of this work as if through all the centuries, far beyond us to those who are yet to come. Hesitatingly it enfolds in the raised arms, and these arms are so heavy that the hand of one already rests again on the top of the head. But the gesture will sleep no more, it collects itself; way up on top of the head, where it is alone, it prepares itself for the labor, for the labor of centuries that has no decline nor end. And in the right foot the first step stands waiting."

* "Never has a human body been so united in its inner being, so controlled by its own soul and again restrained by the elastic power of its blood. And the neck, as it rises a little on the body, which is bent sharply sideways, and stretches and supports the head which listens to the distant pulsations of life, has been so impressively and effectively conceived that one could not imagine a more moving or intensified gesture. It occurs to one that the

Rilke's reference to the great Eleonore Duse as she acted in a D'Annunzio play, indicates once more the poet's own identification of Rodin's works with the spirit of the *Jugendstil* movement.

Two years after the completion of the Rodin book, Rilke undertook a speaking tour in Germany where he gave several highly successful lectures on Rodin. The material for these lectures was compiled, revised in some instances, and published in 1907 as an appendix to the original book. It is significant that, now far removed from the influence of *Jugendstil*, Rilke nevertheless maintained in the revisions the essential spirit of the earlier period. In fact, it is difficult to distinguish the two versions from one another in tone and meaning. For Rilke, in 1902 as well as in 1907, Auguste Rodin demonstrated the fundamental elements of *Jugendstil* in his life and his works. That Rilke was able to recognize this influence and that he never reversed his opinion of it is indeed evidence of the profundity of the poet's attachment to a movement that fascinated him in his early years as a critic.

---

arms are lacking. Rodin perceived them in this case to be too simple a solution to the problem, as something that did not belong to the body which wanted to be wrapped in itself without foreign assistance. One could think of Duse as she (in a play by D'Annunzio), painfully abandoned, tries to embrace without arms and to hold without hands. This scene, in which her body learned a caress which went far beyond it, forms one of the unforgettable memories of her performance. It conveyed the impression that the arms were superfluous, an ornament, a matter of the rich and immoderate, that one could fling them from oneself in order to be totally poor. It was not as if she gave up anything important; rather she gave the impression at this moment of one who gives away his cup in order to drink from the stream, like a person who is naked and yet a bit helpless in his nakedness. It is the same with the armless sculptures of Rodin; nothing essential is lacking. One stands before them as before something whole and perfected that admits to no further additions."

IV: Jugendstil Themes in Rilke's Works

The Insel or New Paradise

In directing attention now to Rilke's own poetic works, it becomes our initial task to define and evaluate those clusters of themes in his writings which, because of their similarity to the ones portrayed in the art of the period, most clearly unite him with the art of *Jugendstil*. This task is not an easy one, especially if one considers the controversy surrounding the definition of a *Jugendstil* theme. Although scholars writing about the period, Elisabeth Klein for example,[1] have devoted much of their efforts to a discussion of typical themes, others, who are more skeptical, have questioned the whole validity of such an approach. They claim rather persuasively that most of the themes supposedly indigenous to this period occur in fact throughout the history of German art and literature. Viewed by themselves, particularly without the further considerations of style and composition, these themes, the skeptics claim, cannot be distinguished from those apparent in several other creative periods of German history.[2] Because of this controversy, it is felt here that any discussion of *Jugendstil* themes in Rilke's works must be undertaken with the greatest of caution. We must be completely aware that only in the fullest of contexts, where all of the elements of style and composition are also taken into consideration, can the complete picture be revealed. With these reservations in mind, let us nevertheless proceed. A subsequent section of our study will concern itself with the details of style and composition that pertain in essence to *Jugendstil*.

One of the most important theme complexes in *Jugendstil* originated in the almost universal alienation from contemporary life which the artists of the movement perceived. They viewed the social, economic, and political developments of their day as threatening their position in society, and they considered the art of their time as cliché-ridden, lifeless, or dull. They asked themselves what their role as artists could be in a time when the industrial machine was destroying the individual and individual creativity and when the insensitive middle classes were dedicated primarily to the acquisition of material goods and to the influence which wealth could provide them. How could they perpetuate an art, they asked, which had relegated itself either to the unaesthetic function of recording social phenomena (as in the case of the naturalists) or to the anachronistic imitation of art forms from the past (as in the case of the historicists)? How were they to maintain themselves and accomplish their aesthetic goals in surroundings which they both despised and feared?

Their response to such a hostile environment was most often a self-imposed exile into a world or enclave of their own creation, into an artistic island, as it were, in which their own special needs and desires could be met. Thus these artists formed small, exclusive circles or "schools" such as the *Insel* group, the Stefan George circle, or the Worpswede colony, where a select few gathered in order to share their common views about the world and about art, to regroup their forces and stimulate each other to creativity, and to develop new ways of artistic expression and fulfillment.

The secluded and subjective, aesthetically oriented, private world of *Jugendstil* found symbolic expression in the so-called *Insel* or island complex of themes. We now realize that the moonlit park landscapes of Ludwig von Hofmann, the medieval castles of Melchior Lechter or Aubrey Beardsley, and the fairy tale or biblical atmosphere of Heinrich Vogeler's works form artistic representations of these artists' isolated, "island" retreats. The exquisite, aesthetic, and even the exotic tone in these works, the tepid pools, the mysterious waterlilies, and the decaying parks all play a role in portraying the "new paradise," as it has been called by Elisabeth Klein.[3] This "island" retreat or "new paradise" is peopled with imaginary medieval knights or saints (perhaps symbolic representations of the artists themselves), with innocent and also voluptuous maidens, and with water sprites or fairies. It is a dreamlike world in which gesture, glance, nuance, and ambience are everything, the blunt word nothing. It possesses a hushed, sanctified air as if one had just entered a holy temple dedicated to the god of art whose prophets the artists viewed themselves to be. Parenthetically, many of the *Jugendstil* artists truly did see themselves as prophets in that sense, and, like Stefan George, gathered disciples for their new religion. Even the highly decorative and ornamental style of *Jugendstil* played a symbolic role in the presentation of the island retreat. As Dolf Sternberger remarks, the *Jugendstil* ornament, although really powerless to ward off the onslaught of the chaotic, threatening environment, nevertheless formed a type of ring within which the artists hoped to conceal themselves. It created, perhaps, a "quiet zone," a "kingdom of beauty," or a "kingdom of the soul" in which the artists could find solitude and live in isolation from the world.[4]

Rilke's earlier works are permeated with the same *Insel* or new paradise theme complex. The poet had long felt strongly alienated from contemporary society, and his association with the artists of the period served as a reinforcement of his isolation while providing him with an artistic form for its expression. A vital element in this theme complex is Rilke's often expressed fear and disdain of modern, bourgeois society and its debilitating effect not only upon himself but upon all that which he considered still pure and undefiled in the world. In the poem "Die Aschanti," for example, he portrays a group of aborigines who had been brought from Africa and were put on display in the Jardin d'Acclimatation in Paris. Their forced stay in the hostile environment of the modern city and their constant exposure to the curiosity of the onlookers had perverted the very essence of their purity, and they became like their observers—lifeless, vain, and grotesquely unappealing:

> Keine Vision von fremden Ländern,
> kein Gefühl von braunen Frauen, die
> tanzen aus den fallenden Gewändern.
>
> Keine wilde fremde Melodie.
> Keine Lieder, die vom Blute stammten,
> und kein Blut, das aus den Tiefen schrie.
>
> Keine braunen Mädchen, die sich samten
> breiteten in Tropenmüdigkeit;
> keine Augen, die wie Waffen flammten,
>
> und die Munde zum Gelächter breit.
> Und ein wunderliches Sich-verstehen
> mit der hellen Menschen Eitelkeit.
>
> Und mir war so bange hinzusehen.*   (SW I, 394–95)

The last line, "And I looked on with such trepidation," conveys the effect that the perverting influence of society has had on the poet himself. It is an unpleasant sight to behold the desecrated purity of the Aschantis. But, more importantly, the poet feels himself threatened by the same force.

In the poem, "Der Einsame," Rilke once more condemns contemporary society, in this instance for its materialism, its smuggness, and its

---

* "No vision of strange lands,/ no sensation of brown women who/ dance out of falling dresses./ No wild, strange melody./ No songs which originate in the blood,/ and no blood crying forth from the depths./ No brown maidens who relax velvetly/ in tropic weariness;/ no eyes which flame like weapons,/ and mouths posed for laughter./ And a peculiar self-awareness/ with the vanity of the white man,/ and I looked on with such trepidation."

insensitivity. He compares his relationship to the modern world with the situation of a lone traveler who has returned home after a long voyage only to find himself a stranger in a highly regulated, closed, and debased environment. He discovers no tolerance or understanding in society for things which are unusual or unknown, and he feels alone, alienated and threatened by it. He longs for a friendlier, more compatible climate:

> Wie einer, der auf fremden Meeren fuhr,
> so bin ich bei den ewig Einheimischen;
> die vollen Tage stehn auf ihren Tischen,
> mir aber ist die Ferne voll Figur.
>
> In mein Gesicht reicht eine Welt herein,
> die vielleicht unbewohnt ist wie ein Mond,
> sie aber lassen kein Gefühl allein,
> und alle ihre Worte sind bewohnt.
>
> Die Dinge, die ich weither mit mir nahm,
> sehn selten aus, gehalten an das Ihre—:
> in ihrer großen Heimat sind sie Tiere,
> hier halten sie den Atem an vor Scham.* (SW I, 393–94)

"Die Ferne" (the distance), the poet's "island world," is as undefiled as the moon, but in the common world: "they leave no emotion alone,/ and all of their words are lived in." Everything is subject to debasement: "in their great homeland they are beasts,/ here they hold their breath in shame."

The insensitivity of modern society which leads it, Rilke believes, to degrade everything with which it has contact is further criticized in a poem from the collection *Mir zur Feier*. Modern man never hesitates to define, categorize, and compartmentalize each element in life so that that element is robbed of its nuance, its life. Even God is debased by the self–righteous burghers. As a result, the poet cries out for the modern world to keep its distance and leave him in peace in his tenuously held "island":

> Ich fürchte mich so vor der Menschen Wort.
> Sie sprechen alles so deutlich aus:

---

* "Like one who has travelled on strange seas,/ I am surrounded by those who never leave home./ The full days stand on their tables,/ but distance is full of meaning for me./ In my gaze a world appears/ which is perhaps as uninhabited as the moon,/ but they leave no emotion alone,/ and all of their words are lived in./ The things which I have brought with me from afar/ appear odd, compared with theirs—:/ in their great homeland they are beasts,/ here they hold their breath in shame."

Und dieses heißt Hund und jenes heißt Haus,
und hier ist Beginn, und das Ende ist dort.

Mich bangt auch ihr Sinn, ihr Spiel mit dem Spott,
sie wissen alles, was wird und war;
kein Berg ist ihnen mehr wunderbar;
ihr Garten und Gut grenzt grade an Gott.

Ich will immer warnen und wehren: Bleibt fern.
Die Dinge singen hör ich so gern.
Ihr rührt sie an: sie sind starr und stumm.
Ihr bringt mir alle die Dinge um.*   (SW III, 257)

In a final example of the theme of alienation, Rilke juxtaposes his "island retreat" once more with the modern world. In his seclusion, he is protected and at home. He finds, however, that if he enters the hostile, contemporary society outside, he will have entered a lifeless, prison-like environment created by man to destroy individuality and creativity:

Und wenn ich abends immer weiterginge
aus meinem Garten, drin ich müde bin, —
ich weiß: dann führen alle Wege hin
zum Arsenal der ungelebten Dinge.
Dort ist kein Baum, als legte sich das Land,
und wie um ein Gefängnis hängt die Wand
ganz fensterlos in siebenfachem Ringe.
Und ihre Tore mit den Eisenspangen,
die denen wehren, welche hinverlangen,
und ihre Gitter sind von Menschenhand.†   (SW I, 317)

In other poems, Rilke concentrated exclusively on a representation of his "island world" or "new paradise" and ignored the disturbing influences from outside. It is not surprising that in these works he

---

* "I am so afraid of people's words./ They express everything so logically,/ and this is a dog and that a house,/ and here is the beginning, and the end is there./ I am terrified also by their meaning, by their game of ridicule./ They know everything that will be and was;/ and no mountain is glorious to them any more;/ and their garden and their land borders even on God./ I always want to protest and warn: 'Stay away!'/ I like so much to hear the things sing./ You trifle with them: they become rigid and silent./ You are going to destroy all of my things."

† "And if I were to go forth in the evening/ from my garden in which I am weary, —/ I know: all paths would lead/ to the arsenal of lifeless things./ There is no tree there, as if nature had ceased to exist,/ and like a prison, the walls/ entirely without windows surround seven times./ And the gates with iron bars/ that hold out those who wish to get in,/ and these bars are made by human hands."

utilized the same symbols and conveyed the same characteristics as his *Jugendstil* associates. The same park or garden landscapes appear, for example, with their majestic swans, their tepid pools of water reflecting the moonlight, their exquisite atmosphere, and their highly decorative style:

> Das sind die Gärten, an die ich glaube:
> Wenn das Blühn in den Beeten bleicht,
> und im Kies unterm löschenden Laube
> lindenleuchtendes Schweigen schleicht.
>
> Auf dem Teich in verrieselnden Ringen
> schwimmt ein Schwan dann von Rand zu Rand.
> Und er wird auf den schimmernden Schwingen
> als Erster die Milde des Mondes bringen
> an den still ersterbenden Strand.* (SW III, 222)

This particular scene is repeated in poem after poem during this period of Rilke's career with much the same tone as can be found in the art of *Jugendstil*. In another example, we read:

> Einmal möcht ich dich wiederschauen,
> Park, mit den alten Lindenalleen.
> . . . .
>
> Schimmernde Schwäne in prahlenden Posen
> gleiten leise auf glänzendem Glatt,
> aus der Tiefe tauchen die Rosen
> wie Sagen einer versunkenen Stadt.
>
> Und wir sind ganz allein im Garten,
> drin die Blumen wie Kinder stehn,
> und wir lächeln und lauschen und warten,
> und wir fragen uns nicht, auf wen . . . † (SW I, 112–13)

Like the artists of the *Jugendstil*, Rilke also portrayed his "island

---

* "Those are the gardens in which I believe:/ when the blooms fade in the flower beds,/ and in the gravel under waning foliage/ the silence illuminating from linden trees creeps./ On the pond, in rippling circles,/ a swan swims then from shore to shore./ And it, on those glistening swirls,/ will be the first to fetch the gentle moon/ for the quietly decaying strand."

† "I would like once again to see you,/ park, with those old linden-lined paths./ . . ./ Glimmering swans in proud poses/ glide softly on glistening smoothness./ From the depths emerge the lilies/ like legends of a lost city./ And we are all alone in the garden,/ where the flowers stand like children,/ and we smile and listen and wait,/ and we don't ask ourselves for whom . . ."

retreat" or "new paradise" symbolically with fortified castles and medieval surroundings. These scenes represented for him as well those desired surroundings which were distant and safe from the intrusion of modern life. Here, in this world of his own choosing, the creative spirit could grow and flourish, and the poet could receive the reward and respect which, as an artist, he felt he so thoroughly deserved:

> . . . ein Schloß an wellenschweren,
> atlasblassen Abendmeeren—
> und in seinen säulenhehren
> Sälen warten Preis und Prunk,
> uns zu ehren:
>
> Weil wir beide wiederkehren—
> ohne Kronen und mit Leeren
> Händen—
> aber jung.*   (SW I, 128)

In the castle, rich rewards and honors await the artists, not because they bear political or worldly power, but because they are "young." (The term "young," in the *Jugendstil* vernacular, connoted all of the positive attributes for which the artists strived, and partially for that reason, became the designation of the period itself.) In another poem, the poet emphasizes the isolation of the castle and also its purity from contact with the outside world, both essential qualities of his "new paradise":

> Ein weißes Schloß in weißer Einsamkeit.
> In blanken Sälen schleichen leise Schauer.
> Todkrank krallt das Gerank sich an die Mauer,
> und alle Wege weltwärts sind verschneit.†   (SW I, 111)

Aside from the symbolic presentation of his personal enclave (the parks and the castles), the poet defines elsewhere rather straightforwardly certain specific and fundamental characteristics which he attributes to this world. It is endowed, for example, with a protective dreamlike quality which acts like a cocoon against the harsh and unpleasant realities of everyday life:

> Mein ganzes Lauschen geht nach innen,
> nicht bis ins Herz stört das Geschwätz,

---

* ". . . a castle on heavy-waved,/ satin-pale, evening seas—/ and in its lofty-pillared/ halls await rewards and splendor/ to honor us:/ because we both return—/ without crowns and with empty/ hands—/ but young."

† "A white castle in pale loneliness./ In bare halls creep faint tremblings./ The vines, deathly ill, cling to the walls,/ and all paths into the world are snowed over."

denn blaue Träume ziehn wie Spinnen
um mich ein selig Wundernetz . . .*   (SW III, 545)

In this protected environment, the poet is allowed to continue his aesthetic reverie undisturbed. It is here, and only here, that he really feels at home:

Ich bin zuhause zwischen Tag und Traum.
Dort wo die Aveglocken grad verklangen
und müde Mädchen mit den warmen Wangen
sich sachte neigen übern Brunnensaum.†   (SW III, 209)

Another of the important qualities which distinguish Rilke's private paradise from the everyday world is the unique and independent temporal order which, he felt, governed it. None of the usual temporal limitations of common life supposedly had validity for or effect on events and their sequence in his private world, for, there, a more exalted order prevailed. In a letter to Lou Andreas-Salomé, a vital companion in Rilke's private paradise, the poet refers to his special temporal realm:

Das war eine von den seltenen Stunden. Solche Stunden sind wie ein dichtumblühtes Inselland: die Wogen athmen ganz leise hinter den Frühlingswällen und kein Nachen kommt aus der Vergangenheit nach und keiner will weiter in die Zukunft.
Daß es dann eine Rückkehr in den Alltag gibt, kann diesen Inselstunden keinen Schaden thun.—Sie bleiben losgelöst von allen andern, wie gelebt in einem zweiten höheren Sein.[5]‡

These "island hours" had no ties with the past nor the future and were in no way affected by the events of everyday surroundings. They existed by and for themselves and possessed their own relevancy in a higher, more meaningful order. Rilke's views concerning the aesthetic necessity of this special temporal realm become evident in a poem written for Heinrich Vogeler. Only in the *Jugendstil* world with its indi-

---

* "All my listening is directed inward,/ and the babble cannot penetrate as far as in my heart,/ because, like spiders, blue dreams/ draw around me a blessed, wonderous web . . ."

† "I feel at home between the day and the dream./ There when the evening bells have just rung/ and weary maidens with glowing faces/ gently lean over the edge of the well."

‡ "That was one of those rare hours. Such hours are like an island thickly surrounded by blooming flowers; the waves breathe very quietly behind these vernal ramparts, and no boat from the past makes its way toward us nor does any seek its way into the future. That there is a return then to the everyday world, cannot harm these 'island' hours—they remain detached from all others and were experienced in a different, more exalted sphere of existence."

vidualistic time reference, it appears, could genuine artistic productivity be anticipated:

> Einsame Stunden sind uns zu eigen,
> wenn das schwere
> tägliche Schweigen
> von uns fällt
> wie ein staubiges Kleid.
> Stimmen hören wir aus unseren Zeiten.
> Denn wir sind wie silberne Geigen
> in den Händen der Ewigkeit.*   (SW III, 636)

The elite group of initiates in the "island enclave" have their own "solitary hours," set apart and distant from the unimportant and lifeless concerns of the common world. There they become the recipients of artistic inspiration and instruments, as it were, in the hands of eternity.

In a poem from the series "Die Parke," Rilke combines in a vivid manner the symbolic park landscape and the concept of a personal temporal order:

> Leise von den Alleen
> ergriffen, rechts and links,
> folgend dem Weitergehen
> irgend eines Winks,
>
> *trittst du mit einem Male*
> in das Beisammensein
> einer schattigen Wasserschale
> mit vier Bänken aus Stein;
>
> *in eine abgetrennte*
> *Zeit, die allein vergeht.*
> Auf feuchte Postamente,
> auf denen nichts mehr steht,
>
> hebst du einen tiefen
> erwartenden Atemzug;
> während das silberne Triefen
> von dem dunkeln Bug
>
> dich schon zu den Seinen
> zählt und weiterspricht.

---

* "Solitary hours especially belong to us,/ when the heavy/ daily silence/ falls from us/ like a dusty cloak./ We then hear voices from our time,/ for we are like silver violins/ in the hands of eternity."

Und du fühlst dich unter Steinen
die hören, und rührst dich nicht.*   (SW I, 603–04; italics mine)

As the poet enters the park, he also enters a distinct, personal world which, in its hushed and expectant tone, obviously has reference to the *Jugendstil* "new paradise." This world is both isolated from the everyday environment and separated from it by a temporal order all its own: "into a detached time/ that elapses on its own."

Rilke's world is further distinguished by the special form of communication, the silence, which prevails there. Rilke's fear of "people's words," quoted earlier, that so bluntly catagorize and compartmentalize each thing, destroying it in the process, will be recalled here. In the poet's personal retreat, the meaningful silence, the fleeting gesture, or at most the utterance of a few hushed words bind the companions together in intimate, exquisite communion with one another and with their surroundings. The sentiments of Maurice Maeterlinck, whom Rilke read and admired greatly, that "la parole est du temps, le silence de l'éternité . . ."[6] ("words are of time, silence of eternity . . .") reflect Rilke's own thinking on the subject. He himself stated the following in a short essay entitled "Der Wert des Monologes": "Aber man wird einmal aufhören müssen, '*das Wort*' zu überschätzen. Man wird einsehen lernen, daß es nur eine von den vielen Brücken ist, die das Eiland unserer Seele mit dem großen Kontinent des gemeinsamen Lebens verbinden, die breiteste vielleicht, aber keineswegs die feinste. . . . Man wird es deshalb aufgeben, von den Worten Aufschlüsse über die Seele zu erwarten . . ." (SW V, 435).† Interesting in our context is the poet's use of the metaphors "island" and "continent" to distinguish the separation and isolation of the soul (read *Jugendstil* artist) from the common world. Later in the same essay, Rilke associates words with the common occurrences of everyday life, but he distinguishes meaningful silence as having to do with those most fundamental and essential experiences of the soul:

Aber es giebt Mächtigeres als Taten und Worte. Diese sind endlich nur das, womit wir teilnehmen an dem gemeinsamen Alltag. . . . Wir hätten sie kaum

---

* "Softly enchanted by the/ paths, right and left, and/ pursuing the passage of/ some indefinite wave of the hand,/ *you enter suddenly*/ the presence/ of a shadowy fountain/ with four benches of stone;/ *into a detached time*/ *that elapses on its own*./ On wet pedestals/ on which nothing more stands,/ you heave a deep,/ expectant sigh;/ while the silvery drops/ from the dark bend/ already count you as/ one of their own and go on speaking./ And you feel that you are among/ stones that hear, and you do not stir."

† "Sometime, we shall have to stop over-evaluating the word. We shall learn to realize that it is only one of the many bridges that connect the island of our soul with the great

gebraucht, wenn wir Einsame geblieben wären, . . . und wir brauchen sie in der Tat night in den Augenblicken, da wir uns so einsam fühlen. Dann sind wir eines leiseren Erlebens voll, heimgekehrt in ein Land mit heiligen, heimlichen Gebräuchen, schöpferisch in aller Untätigkeit und den Worten entwachsen (SW V, 436).*

Throughout Rilke's works, as a result of his preoccupation with silence, words such as "schweigsam" (silent), "leise" (hushed), and "lauschen" (listening) appear. In much of his writing, silence itself also becomes an important theme. A particularly interesting poem on this theme combines specific autobiographical references to the exclusive Worpswede group's Sunday evening gatherings and the poet's silent means of communication with the members of that group:

> Ich bin bei euch, ihr Sonntagabendlichen.
> Mein Leben ist beglänzt und überglüht.
> Ich rede zwar; doch, mit dem sonst verglichen,
> sind alle Worte jetzt von mir gewichen,
> und meine Schweigsamkeit steht auf und blüht . . .
>
> Denn das sind Lieder: schönes Schweigen vieler,
> das aus dem einen wie in Strahlen steigt.
> . . . .
> Ich bin bei euch, ihr sanfren Aufmerksamen.
> Ihr seid die Säulen meiner Einsamkeit.†   (SW III, 704)

The "Sunday-evening-ones" and the "attentive ones" are undoubtedly the "girls in white," Paula Becker and Clara Westhoff as well as the other sympathetic artists at Worpswede, who felt, understood, and shared his "silence." In an earlier poem, Rilke found cause to admonish himself to be more "silent" than he had been recently in order to expand the limits of his being. Through his "Lauschen" (listening) and his "Staunen"

---

continent of common life, the broadest perhaps, but in no way the most refined. . . . We shall therefore give up expecting words to provide us with information about the soul . . ."

* "There are more powerful things than deeds and words. These are in the last analysis only the means by which we take part in the common everyday life. . . . We would hardly need them if we had remained apart, . . . and we do not need them in fact in those moments when we feel so solitary. We are then full of a subtler experience and have returned home to a land with holy and secret customs which in their inactivity create and have outgrown the need for words."

† "I am with you, you Sunday-evening-ones./ My soul is glittered and glowing./ I speak, to be sure, but all of the/ usual words have dissipated from me/ and my silence springs forth and blossoms . . . / For these are truly songs: the beautiful silence of many/ that rises united as in rays./ . . . / I am with you, you softly attentive ones./ You are the pillars of my solitude."

(wonderment), he hoped he would be more able to commune with the elements of his island surroundings and derive from this meditation a rebirth of his spirit:

> Vor lauter Lauschen und Staunen sei still,
> du mein tieftiefes Leben;
> daß du weißt, was der Wind dir will,
> eh noch die Birken beben.
>
> . . . .
>
> Und dann meine Seele sei weit, sei weit,
> daß dir das Leben gelinge,
> breite dich wie ein Feierkleid
> über die sinnenden Dinge.* (SW III, 212)

In the final example selected here from many similar poems, Rilke once more compares his own private world with the unpleasant common one. In his own surroundings, the voices are tranquil, but in the outside world, which he describes as "a meaningless and fearful time," there is no quietude:

> Denn dann nur sind die Stimmen gut,
> wenn Schweigsamkeiten sie begleiten,
>
> . . . .
>
> und bang und sinnlos sind die Zeiten,
> wenn hinter ihren Eitelkeiten
> nicht etwas waltet, welches ruht.† (SW I, 427)

The hushed, exquisite atmosphere of the poems above conveys, as in many others of the period, distinct overtones of a worshipful reverence. The "sanctified" or "sacred" air of many of Rilke's works forms an additional fundamental characteristic of the poet's *Insel* theme complex. Again, Rilke's writing corresponds to traits prevalent throughout *Jugendstil*. The contempt these artists felt for the common world was caused in part by the fact that the artist had lost his position of respect in society. No longer was he thought to be the prophet, philosopher, or sage to whom all the world looked for guidance and direction. Within the confines of their isolated "islands," therefore, the artist was again restored to his earlier position of respect. The major difficulty in achiev-

---

* "In utter perception and wonderment be silent/ my deep, deep soul;/ that you may know what the wind wants with you/ before even the birches begin to tremble./ . . ./ And then, my soul, expand to vastness/ that your life might succeed;/ spread yourself like a festive cloak/ over the pondering things."

† "For voices are worthwhile only then/ when they are accompanied by silence,/ . . . / fearful and meaningless are those times/ when behind the vanity/ nothing governs that is still."

ing such a restoration arose, however, in the realization that the traditional aesthetic, religious, and ethical systems, upon which artists of the past had so heavily relied, no longer seemed valid or believable, especially to the representatives of *Jugendstil*. It was impossible at this point to restore, even in the "new paradise," the earlier circumstances in which artists could be the proponents of "the Good, the True, and the Beautiful." In place of these "anachronistic" systems, according to Horst Fritz, the artists of *Jugendstil* created their own new faith and produced their own new type of religious fervor. The object of their devotion and worship became their art.[7] As a result, the elitist circles of *Jugendstil* assumed the attributes of a religious cult, their gatherings the air of a mystical divine service, their meeting places became temples to art, and most importantly, the artists themselves became the prophets and priests of the new religion. Rilke's views in this regard were typical. In a short essay concerning the latest art events in Berlin, entitled "Die neue Kunst in Berlin," Rilke demonstrated very early in his writing career an inclination to deify art. In reference to the owners of the then avant-garde art gallery Keller & Reiner, the poet states:

Und sie haben ein großes Verdienst, die beiden jungen mutigen Besitzer, die dem Neuen *eine Kirche* bauen mitten unter den Ungläubigen oder Glaubensschwachen. Sie tun mehr als das Libertyhaus für London oder Bing für Paris getan hat: sie wagen. Und mögen sie nun gewinnen oder nicht, man wird sie nicht vergessen dürfen.

Aber ich glaube, es ist bald Zeit, auch in Österreich und in Deutschland. Allenthalben erwachen *wahre und ernste Apostel der Schönheit. Und sie predigen das Heil und nennen den Namen Gottes in neuen Sprachen* (SW V, 446; italics mine).*

Indeed Rilke looked upon himself as one of the "apostles of beauty" and his works reflect this orientation. His mention, by the way, of the famous Liberty House and of Bing's work in Paris indicates once more Rilke's complete familiarity with the development of *Jugendstil* even in its European context.

The resultant reverent, "sanctified" tone of his writing forms the basis particularly for Rilke's *Stunden-Buch*. This is so much the case that some critics in the past have considered the work to be a sort of a collection of Christian prayers by a devout poet. From the *Jugendstil* frame

---

* "And they have accomplished much these two young and courageous owners who are building, among disbelievers or those with weak faith, *a church* for that which is new. They are doing more than the Liberty House did for London or Bing for Paris, for they are willing to take risks. And whether they win or not, we shall not be able to forget them. But I believe that it will soon be about time for Austria and Germany. On all sides *arise true and serious apostles of beauty. And they preach the gospel and call out the name of God in new languages.*"

of reference, however, it becomes obvious that even though the poet utilized many Christian symbols and metaphors throughout the work his real intent is far removed from that tradition.[8] Especially in the first section, *Vom mönchischen Leben*, the poet-monk sets out in his search for the god of art. This god appears at times to be all-powerful and terrible in his greatness; on other occasions, he is weak, helpless, and dependent on the poet. The poet is in some poems a humble supplicant and fully reliant on the god of art for inspiration:

> Du bist so groß, daß ich schon nicht mehr bin,
> wenn ich mich nur in deine Nähe stelle.
> Du bist so dunkel; meine kleine Helle
> an deinem Saum hat keinen Sinn.
> Dein Wille geht wie eine Welle
> und jeder Tag ertrinkt darin.*   (SW I, 269)

But at times, the poet becomes the god's only means of survival:

> Du, Nachbar Gott, wenn ich dich manchesmal
> in langer Nacht mit hartem Klopfen störe,—
> so ists, weil ich dich selten atmen höre
> und weiß: Du bist allein im Saal.
> . . . .
> Ich horche immer. Gieb ein kleines Zeichen.
> Ich bin ganz nah.†   (SW I, 255)

There are moments in *Stunden-Buch* when the poet-monk is in direct communion with his god, and when he feels that he might be approaching the capability of capturing god's presence in his works:

> Ich bin, du Ängstlicher. Hörst du mich nicht
> mit allen meinen Sinnen an dir branden?
> Meine Gefühle, welche Flügel fanden,
> umkreisen weiß dein Angesicht.
> Siehst du nicht meine Seele, wie sie dicht
> vor dir in einem Kleid aus Stille steht?
> Reift nicht mein mailiches Gebet
> an deinem Blicke wie an einem Baum?‡   (SW I, 264)

* "You are so great that I no longer exist,/ if I put myself in your presence./ You are so dark, my tiny illumination/ has no meaning in your vicinity./ Your will flows like a wave/ and every day drowns in it."

† "You, Neighbor God, if I sometimes/ disturb you in the long night by my hard knocking,/ it is because I so seldom hear you breathing/ and know that you are alone in your room./ . . ./ I listen always. Give me a small sign./ I'm quite near."

‡ "I am, you fearful one. Don't you hear me/ surging with all my senses against you?/ My emotions, which discovered wings,/ circle in white your countenance./ Don't you see my

In other poems, he humbly submits himself anew to his god in a penitent voice:

> Ich bete wieder, du Erlauchter,
> du hörst mich wieder durch den Wind,
> weil meine Tiefen niegebrauchter
> rauschender Worte mächtig sind.
>
> Ich war zerstreut; an Widersacher
> in Stücken war verteilt mein Ich.
> O Gott, mich lachten alle Lacher
> und alle Trinker tranken mich.
>
> . . . .
>
> Jetzt bin ich wieder aufgebaut
> aus allen Stücken meiner Schande,
> und sehne mich nach einem Bande,
> nach einem einigen Verstande,
> der mich wie *ein* Ding überschaut,—
> nach deines Herzens großen Händen—
> (o kämen sie doch auf mich zu).
> Ich zähle mich, mein Gott, und du,
> du hast das Recht, mich zu verschwenden.*   (SW I, 306–07)

Not only in *Stunden-Buch*, however, do we discover the search for the god of art of *Jugendstil* and the "sacred" and worshipful atmosphere; it runs through all of Rilke's early works. In his "island" world, Rilke was indeed the prophet, priest, or "apostle of beauty," and his mission as such was to proclaim the new gospel of art, at least to the initiates. In another example from a poem to Vogeler, he writes:

> Wir sind uns oft in *einem* Gotte nah.
> Ich denke dann: Wir Schaffenden sind da,
> um diesen Größten mächtig zu verkünden.
> Und oft wenn wir uns zueinander neigen
> geschieht mir wieder: daß wir uns verbünden
> um seine Wunder würdig zu verschweigen.†   (SW III, 635)

---

soul as it closely/ stands before you in a cloak of silence?/ Doesn't my spring-like prayer/ ripen on your glances as on a tree?"

* "I am praying again, you Most Holy One,/ you can hear me again on the wind/ because these depths of mine proclaim/ rushing words that were never used before./ I was confused; my being was/ divided by adversaries into pieces./ O God, I was laughed by all those who made merry/ and drunk by all those who drank./ . . ./ Now I am united again/ from all the pieces of my shame/ and long for a tie/ with a single intellect/ that comprehends me like a *thing*—/ I long for the great hands of your heart—/ (O might they come towards me)./ I count myself, my God, and you,/ you have the right to expend me."

† "We are often near to one another in *one* God./ I think then: we creators exist/ in order

The "Czar" poems, particularly the last three dealing with the young Fedor V (which Rilke originally composed in 1899 after his first Russian visit), seem especially expressive of a worshipful tone as well as the other attributes of the poet's *Jugendstil* "island" world, and as such may serve here as a summary to our discussion. First of all, there is the ornate setting at the Russian court with its knights, princes, and emperor. Secondly, a confrontation with a new and threatening age occurs along with the typical withdrawal inward from the hostile world. Finally, there is the sensitive and aesthetic young emperor himself who is endowed with all the sacred attributes of priest and prophet. All of this is treated in the highly decorative style of *Jugendstil*.

In the first of these three poems, we discover the young Czar sitting on his magnificent throne in his imperial robes. Before him in the large hall, a loud and boisterous festival is in progress in which he seems to have very little interest. Having only recently been crowned emperor and being slight and even delicate in stature, he stands in great contrast to the physically overpowering forebears who have preceded him to the throne. Despite this disparity, he still carries the last vestiges of their power, but the princes of the land, the *Bojaren*, would be only too happy to take it from him at the least sign of weakness:

> Der blasse Zar, des Stammes letztes Glied,
> träumt auf dem Thron, davor das Fest geschieht,
> und leise zittert sein beschämter Scheitel
> und seine Hand, die vor den Purpurlehnen
> mit einem unbestimmten Sehnen
> ins wirre Ungewisse flieht.
>
> Und um sein Schweigen neigen sich Bojaren
> in blanken Panzern und in Pantherfellen,
> wie viele fremde fürstliche Gefahren,
> die ihn mit stummer Ungeduld umstellen.
> Tief in den Saal schlägt ihre Ehrfurcht Wellen.
>
> Und sie gedenken eines andern Zaren,
> . . . .
> Und denken also weiter: *jener* ließ
> nicht so viel Raum, wenn er zu Throne saß,
> auf dem verwelkten Samt des Kissens leer.
> . . . .
> Und weiter denken sie: das Kaiserkleid

---

mightily to proclaim this Greatest One./ And often when we bow toward one another/ it comes to me again that we are united/ in order worthily to keep secret His wonders."

schläft auf den Schultern dieses Knaben ein.
Obgleich im ganzen Saal die Fackeln flacken,
sind bleich die Perlen, die in sieben Reihn,
wie weiße Kinder, knien um seinen Nacken,
und die Rubine an den Ärmelzacken,
die einst Pokale waren, klar von Wein,
sind schwarz wie Schlacken—*   (SW I, 432–33)

The Czar's only hope for survival lies in the traditions of power represented by the magnificence of his ornate surroundings: the throne, the
robes and the jewels; but he can also retreat into his own world of
dreams. By such a retreat, he can hide behind an inscrutable, uncommunicative countenance, he can hide his real weakness from the princes.
Because of the barrier created by his silence, he, at least for the time
being, maintains himself and receives the temporary though hollow
adulation of his subjects:

Es drängt sich heftig an den blassen Kaiser,
auf dessen Haupt die Krone immer leiser
und dem der Wille immer fremder wird;
er lächelt. Lauter prüfen ihn die Preiser,
ihr Neigen nähert sich, sie schmeicheln heiser
und eine Klinge hat im Traum geklirrt.†   (SW I, 433)

We are assured in the next poem that despite the threat of the
Boyars the young Czar will survive: this primarily because he has been
sanctified by his "distant longing," another term perhaps for his "holy"
calling:

Der blasse Zar wird nicht am Schwerte sterben,
die fremde Sehnsucht macht ihn sakrosankt;

---

* "The pale Czar, the last member of his family,/ dreams on the throne before which the
celebration takes place/ and softly his shamed head trembles/ and his hand, which flees
before the purple armrests/ with an uncertain longing/ into confused uncertainty./ And the
Boyars bow around his silence/ in shiny armor and in panther skins/ like many strange
princely perils/ that surround him with dumb impatience./ Deep into the hall the waves of
their reverence flow./ And they remember another Czar./ . . ./ And they think further: *that*
Czar did not/ leave as much room, whenever he sat on the throne,/ on the faded silk of the
cushion./ . . ./ And they think further: The imperial robes/ fall asleep on the shoulders of
this boy./ Although in the whole hall the torches flicker,/ the pearls are pale which in seven
rows/ like white children kneel around his neck,/ and the rubies on the arm-clasps,/ which
once were like goblets clear with wine,/ are now black as cinders—"

† "They press forward forcefully toward the pale emperor/ on whose head the crown gets
softer and softer/ and whose will becomes more and more distant./ He smiles. The praisers
survey him louder,/ their bows draw nearer, and they flatter more hoarsely/ and a sword
rattled in his dream."

er wird die feierlichen Reiche erben,
an denen seine sanfte Seele krankt.*   (SW I, 433)

In the final poem of the series, we receive a glimpse of the true
splendor of the Czar's isolated world and of his truly sanctified and holy
position in this world. Here, in his "priestly" robes, he stands before an
icon which is described with the typical *Jugendstil* ornateness and is
somewhat reminiscent of the undulating line:

> Noch immer schauen in den Silberplatten
> wie tiefe Frauenaugen die Saphire,
> Goldranken schlingen sich wie schlanke Tiere,
> die sich im Glanze ihrer Brünste gatten,
> und sanfte Perlen warten in dem Schatten
> wilder Gebilde, daß ein Schimmer ihre
> stillen Gesichter finde und verliere.
> Und das ist Mantel, Strahlenkranz und Land,
> und ein Bewegen geht von Rand zu Rand,
> wie Korn im Wind und wie ein Fluß im Tale,
> so glänzt es wechselnd durch die Rahmenwand.†

The Czar then bows before the icon and prays:

> Fühltest Du nicht, wie sehr wir in Dich drangen
> mit allem Fühlen, Fürchten und Verlangen:
> wir warten auf Dein liebes Angesicht,
> das uns vergangen ist; wohin vergangen?:
>
> Den großen Heiligen vergeht es nicht.‡

The expected result of the prayer of one so holy ensues:

> Er bebte tief in seinem steifen Kleid,
> das strahlend stand. Er wußte nicht, wie weit

---

* "The pale Czar will not die of the sword,/ his distant longing makes him sacrosanct;/ he
will inherit the festive empires/ on which his gentle soul perishes."

† "Still the saphires watch/ in the silver plates like deep eyes of women./ Gold filigree
entwines like slender beasts/ who mate in the splendor of their passion,/ and soft pearls
wait in the shadow/ of wild designs for a glimmer to find/ and lose their still faces./ And all
this is a mantle, a crown, a kingdom,/ and movement permeates from border to border/
like corn in the wind and like a stream in the valley;/ thus it shines alternatively in the
framework."

‡ "Didn't you feel how very much we penetrated to you/ with all of our feeling, our fear-
ing and our desiring:/ we wait for your beloved countenance/ that has left us—whereto?/ It
never leaves the great saints."

er schon von allem war, und ihrem Segnen
wie selig nah in seiner Einsamkeit.*

Finally, through continued contemplation and devotion, he finds the
hoped for mystical union between himself and the god represented by
the icon, and they, in their equal splendor, become one:

Noch sinnt und sinnt der blasse Gossudar.
Und sein Gesicht, das unterm kranken Haar
schon lange tief und wie im Fortgehn war,
verging, wie jenes in dem Goldovale,
in seinem großen goldenen Talar.
. . . .
Zwei Goldgewänder schimmerten im Saale
und wurden in dem Glanz der Ampeln klar.†   (SW I, 435–36)

The autobiographical and *Jugendstil* allusions are quite obvious. The
Czar, or the artist-priest, in his precarious but solitary personal world,
sets out to discover and commune with the icon or the god of art.
Because of his sanctity and devotion, he is successful in his goal. In his
own world, the Czar (or the artist-priest) attains what, of course, he
never could in the mundane world. He reaches a position of true
supremacy and superiority and finds union with his diety.

Geist und Leben: The Dichotomy of an Age

The artists of *Jugendstil* not only felt themselves at odds with modern society and their surroundings in general, they also recognized a
fundamental dichotomy in their age. On the one hand, they had the
profound impression of being at the end of an era and discerned around
them and within themselves a decline in vigor, ambition, and a growing
sense of melancholia. On the other hand, these artists perceived a
distinct need for a renewal of their artistic energies and a rejuvenation of
the forces of life, and they set as their goal the realization of a new and

---

* "He trembled deeply in his stiff cloak/ that stood radiantly. He didn't know how distant/
he already was from everything and how/ blessedly near in his solitude to her blessing."

† "And still the pale Czar contemplates and contemplates./ And his face which, under sick
hair,/ has long been deep and about to leave,/ departs like the other one in the golden oval/
in his great, golden robe./ . . ./ Two golden robes shimmered in the room/ and became clear
in the glow of the lamps."

revitalized age. There were among these artists in the various *Jugendstil* circles notorious dandies such as Oscar Wilde, Aubrey Beardsley, and Alfred Walter Heymel with his "green, silken Japanese vest with the silver embroidery" as well as the theorists and activists such as Henry van de Velde, Hermann Obrist, and some members of the Worpswede group.[9] There were also artists such as Heinrich Vogeler who manifested both vitality and decadence. Not only was Vogeler the chief illustrator of the exquisitely decadent *Insel* publications and the companion and admirer of Heymel and Rudolf Alexander Schröder, he also became a major force in the movement toward a return to nature, a renewed vigor and an harmonious existence with the forces of life. As a further development of these latter tendencies, he eventually founded the Worpswede workers' commune and some years thereafter even emigrated to Russia where he dedicated his work to the furtherance of the communist cause. Many of the artists were what Hugo von Hofmannsthal described as "frühgereift und zart und traurig" ("precocious and fragile and melancholy"),[10] but they were also the first ones to call for a vitalistic rebirth and a reunification of life and art with the primordial forces of the universe.

The works of *Jugendstil* demonstrate the all-pervasiveness of the dichotomy, for they often convey both a tone of resignation, decadence, and lifeless intellectualism (*Geist*) as well as a spirit of energy, vitalism, and a rebirth of life's forces (*Leben*). Thus the typical *Jugendstil* work is fraught with an underlying tension, and although the artists undertook, in many instances, to synthesize in their art and in their lives the two opposing forces, their solutions were usually very tenuous indeed. What they hoped would evolve into an harmonious fusion of opposites remained very much the same deep, internal polarization.

The young Rainer Maria Rilke, like the other artists of his time, could hardly have been impervious to the disharmonies of his age, particularly considering his own background in conservative and traditional Austria and his complete submersion then in the modernist ideas of the avant-garde in Munich, Berlin and elsewhere. He too responded to the seemingly unbridgeable chasm between *Geist* and *Leben* by incorporating it as one of the major theme complexes of his *Jugendstil* works.

One of the pronounced variations on the theme—the contrast between *Lebensmüdigkeit*, or weariness with life, and vitalism, or a pulsating resurgence of strength and energy—can be detected throughout his writings of the period. Rilke had the habit during his early life (and occasionally even later) of claiming that he was the descendant of an old line of nobility which had slowly died out, losing its wealth and influence. As one of its last members, he was left with only the noble inclinations but none of the means or the strength to restore it to its earlier glory. We know, of course, that Rilke's noble lineage was entirely imaginary; nevertheless, this pretention served as a convenient fiction with which he could portray the inheritors of a dying age. As such it formed the basis for a considerable number of Rilke's works. In such works we usually discover a noble family gradually degenerating and the last member, tired and weak, succumbing to total pessimism and ruin. These poems express allegorically one side of the polarity between *Leben* and *Geist*, the *Lebensmüdigkeit*, and represent the wide-spread feelings of malaise so prevalent in the *Jugendstil* period.

"Der Letzte," from *Das Buch der Bilder*, is such a poem. The main figure, perhaps the poet himself, laments the passage of his family's influence and strength but resignedly accepts the hopelessness of his own situation. He is physically weary, mentally and spiritually bankrupt, and he sees his only role in life now as endurance until his end:

> Mit drei Zweigen hat mein Geschlecht geblüht
> auf sieben Schlössern im Wald,
> und wurde seines Wappens müd
> und war schon viel zu alt;—
> und was sie mir ließen und was ich erwerbe
> zum alten Besitze, ist heimatlos.
> In meinen Händen, in meinem Schooß
> muß ich es halten, bis ich sterbe.
> Denn was ich fortstelle,
> hinein in die Welt,
> fällt,
> ist wie auf eine Welle
> gestellt.*   (SW I, 395–96)

In another poem, the same tone persists, with the similar context of an old, once powerful family now degenerate, whose last member has been left melancholy, weak, and without hope for the future:

> Das ist der Tag, in dem ich traurig throne,
> . . . .
> da bet ich: daß ich einmal meine Krone
> von meinem Haupte heben darf.

---

* "My family blossomed with three branches/ in seven castles in the forest,/ and became tired of its coat of arms/ and was already much too old;—/ and what they left me, and what I might add/ to the old possessions, is without a resting place./ I must hold it in my hands/ and in my lap until I die./ For that which I perpetuate/ in the world/ will fall/ and is placed/ as if on a wave."

Lang muß ich ihrem dumpfen Drucke dienen,
darf ich zum Dank nicht einmal ihren blaun
Türkisen, ihren Rauten und Rubinen
erschauernd in die Augen schaun?

Vielleicht erstarb schon lang der Strahl der Steine,
. . . .
vielleicht auch waren in der Krone keine,
die ich bekam? . . .*   (SW I, 150)

The heavy and burdensome crown has lost its luster and the persona
doubts in the last line if it has ever had any. He continues to bear the
unrewarding obligations of rule, although he, like the crown, has lost all
splendor and would gladly free himself from his responsibilities. But he
has no energy left for a change and thus accepts his role with quiet
resignation.

In one of the Czar poems, Fedor ("The pale Czar"), presents a
variation on this theme in that a modicum of comfort, but no solution, is
found even in the hopeless fatigue and resignation of those, like the
Jugendstil artists, who preside over the end of an age. After looking from
his Kremlin window at the magnificent architectural accomplishment of
his ancestors and the great power they had assembled and after considering his own ineffectiveness, weakness and weariness, there at first
seems nothing left for Fedor but despair. Suddenly, however, a new
sensation begins to well up within him, and he begins to understand the
reason for his weakness, that there is purpose for it and an order to life
after all, that it has come about for a good cause:

Und er begreift auf einmal, wer sie waren,
und daß sie oft um ihres Dunkels Sinn
in *seine* eignen Tiefen niedertauchten
und ihn, den Leisesten von den Erlauchten,
in ihren Taten groß und fromm verbrauchten
schon lang vor seinem Anbeginn.

Und eine Dankbarkeit kommt über ihn,
daß sie ihn so verschwenderisch vergeben
an aller Dinge Durst und Drang.
Er war die Kraft zu ihrem Überschwang,

* "That is the day in which I sadly reign,/ . . ./ and I pray that sometime I be permitted/ to
lift the crown from my head./ I shall long have to serve its stifling weight;/ may I not in
thankfulness at some time/ see, trembling with my own eyes,/ its blue turquoise, its
diamonds, and its rubies?/ Perhaps the stones have already lost their glimmer,/ . . ./
perhaps there were none in the crown/ which I received? . . ."

der goldne Grund, vor dem ihr breites Leben
geheimnisvoll zu dunkeln schien.

In allen ihren Werken schaut er *sich*,
wie eingelegtes Silber in Zieraten,
und es giebt keine Tat in ihren Taten,
die nicht auch *war* in seinen stillen Staaten,
in denen alles Handelns Rot verblich.*   (SW I, 434)

His ancestors were so vigorous primarily because they had his and their
other descendants' strength to draw upon, and in their deeds, they
consumed the life's force of all those who came after them. Without the
pale Czar, they would never have succeeded; in effect then, he too contributed a vital part to their glory. For this thought he is thankful.

In other works, not necessarily associated with the theme of the
degenerating family, the same tone of weariness with life appears. The
famous poem "Herbsttag" is one such example. The last stanza reads:

Wer jetzt kein Haus hat, baut sich keines mehr.
Wer jetzt allein ist, wird es lange bleiben,
wird wachen, lesen, lange Briefe schreiben
und wird in den Alleen hin und her
unruhig wandern, wenn die Blätter treiben.†   (SW I, 398)

The uneventful activities of reading, writing letters, and wandering
about the avenues represent pastimes which people generally undertake in their final years of life when new projects hardly seem worthwhile starting. That Rilke composed the poem at such an early age, yet
fully captured the resignation and submission to life of old age, points to
his very strong feelings of *Lebensmüdigkeit*. In another poem, the mood is
even more despondent:

Ich sehe seit einer Zeit,
wie alles sich verwandelt.
Etwas steht auf und handelt
und tötet und tut Leid.

* "And he comprehends suddenly who they were/ and that they often in their dark
purposes/ submerged themselves in *his* own depths/ and used him, the stillest of the noble
ones,/ for their great and pious deeds,/ long before his beginning./ And thankfulness
comes over him/ that they squandered him/ in their craving and thirst for all things./ He
was the strength of their conquering,/ the golden ground, before which their expansive
lives/ seemed mysteriously to grow dim./ In all of their works he sees *himself*,/ like inlaid
silver in fine ornamentation,/ and there is no deed among all of theirs/ which was not also
in his quiet being/ where now the redness of action has paled."

† "Whoever has no house now, will not build one./ Who is alone now, will stay that way

Von Mal zu Mal sind all
die Gärten nicht dieselben;
von den gilbenden zu der gelben
langsamem Verfall:
wie war der Weg mir weit.

Jetzt bin ich bei den leeren
und schaue durch alle Alleen.
Fast bis zu den fernen Meeren
kann ich den ernsten schweren
verwehrenden Himmel sehn.*   (SW I, 399–400)

In the same period in which the works quoted above appeared,
Rilke wrote many poems, essays, and passages in his diaries in which a
vitalistic spirit reigns, in which a resurgence of life and a hope for the
future prevails. In these works, where the other aspect of the polarity,
Leben, is predominant, Rilke reflects similar ideas to those he attributed
to Vogeler in the latter's retreat to the soil and to the simple, unadorned
life of Worpswede. Rilke's feelings, as expressed in these works, convey
above all his intense search for a renewed unity with the vital forces of
life. In that respect, they are reminiscent of his comments concerning
other artists of the period, van de Velde, for example: "Das ist das
Merkwürdige: bei dem Belgier wirkt sogar jede seltene Verzierung organisch, wie von innen heraus. Als ob das Ding an einer Stelle etwas von
seiner tieferen seelischen Schönheit verriete, so ist jede Falte, jeder
Messingteil" (SW V, 444–45).† In Rilke's opinion, it was van de Velde's
great achievement that he was able to commune with the "soul" of life
and to understand its needs, that he allowed each of his creations to
reveal its innermost being and its deepest beauty. In a passage from his
diary, he expressed the wish to establish the same sort of unity with life:

In jedem Ding will ich eine Nacht ruhn, wenn ich am Tage mit meinem Tun
durch die anderen Dinge ging.—Bei jedem Ding will ich einmal schlafen, von
seiner Wärme müd werden, auf seinen Atemzügen auf und nieder träumen,
seine liebe gelöste nackte Nachbarschaft an allen meinen Gliedern spüren und

---

for a long time,/ will watch, read, write long letters/ and will wander restlessly about on
the avenues/ when the leaves are blown to and fro by the wind."

* "For some time, I have noticed/ how everything changes./ Something rises up and acts/
and kills and causes suffering./ From one time to the next,/ the gardens are not the same;/
from the yellowing ones to the ones already yellow in their slow decay:/ how long the path
has been for me./ Now I am with the empty ones/ and can see up and down the avenues./
Almost to the distant seas/ I can see the earnest, heavy/ forbidding heavens."

† "That is the remarkable thing: in the Belgian's work, every unusual ornamentation has

stark werden durch den Duft seines Schlafes und dann am Morgen früh, eh es erwacht, vor allem Abschied, weitergehen, weitergehen . . .[11*]

In one poem from *Das Buch der Bilder*, the poet realizes that a re-unification with life can only occur if he forgets the "civilized" habit of analyzing and ordering his surroundings and completely subjugates himself to the will of nature. He comprehends the insignificance of ordinary human concerns when compared to the forces of life, yet he recognizes that these same human concerns keep mankind from communion with life:

> Wie ist das klein, womit wir ringen,
> was mit uns ringt, wie ist das groß;
> ließen wir, ähnlicher den Dingen,
> uns *so* vom großen Sturm bezwingen,—
> wir würden weit und namenlos.
>
> Was wir besiegen, ist das Kleine,
> und der Erfolg selbst macht uns klein.
> Das Ewige und Ungemeine
> *will* nicht von uns gebogen sein.† (SW I, 459)

If, like the "things," man could forget himself and his desire to conquer his surroundings, he could become "vast" and "nameless," terms which signify the unity for which Rilke was striving.

In two other poems, Rilke records those periods in his life when he felt life pulsating through his veins and himself in full harmony with his surroundings. In these times, the melancholia of the earlier works has totally disappeared and the dawning of a new age appears close at hand:

> Und wieder rauscht mein tiefes Leben lauter,
> als ob es jetzt in breitern Ufern ginge.
> Immer verwandter werden mir die Dinge

---

an organic effect, as if it grew from the inside outward. It is as if this one specific spot revealed something of the deeper spiritual beauty of the object. So it is with each crease and with each brass part."

* "I would like to rest a night in each thing whenever I rush through the other things during my daily activity. I want to sleep near each thing once, become tired through its warmth, in dreams rise and fall on its breath, feel its precious, liberated, naked nearness on all the limbs of my body and become strong through the fragrance of its sleep. And then in the morning early, before it awakens, before it can say goodbye, I want to go on . . ."

† "How insignificant is that with which we struggle,/ and that which struggles with us, how great;/ if we, more similar to the things,/ would let ourselves be subdued by the great storm,/ we would become vast and nameless./ That which we conquer is trivial/ and the success itself makes us trivial too./ That which is uncommon and eternal/ will not allow us to triumph over it."

und alle Bilder immer angeschauter.
Dem Namenlosen fühl ich mich vertrauter:
Mit meinen Sinnen, wie mit Vögeln, reiche
ich in die windigen Himmel aus der Eiche,
und in den abgebrochnen Tag der Teiche
sinkt, wie auf Fischen stehend, mein Gefühl.*　　　　　(SW I, 402)

In the second example, in which he specifically mentions his unification with the "holy harmony," he again responds to the surging life within him:

Das sind die Stunden, da ich mich finde.
Dunkel wellen die Wiesen im Winde,
allen Birken schimmert die Rinde,
und der Abend kommt über sie.

Und ich wachse im reichen Schweigen,
möchte blühen mit hundert Zweigen,
nur um mit allen mich tief zu neigen
vor der heiligen Harmonie . . . †　　　　　(SW III, 254)

In a final example of this aspect of the *Leben*-and-*Geist* dichotomy, Rilke once more states his hopes of attaining the goal of his search and perceives success. He notes that the "unity with the things" will be the only means for his overcoming what he calls the "ultimate fear," a term used here to express the uncertainties of his dying age:

Und dieses, welches ganz unwillkürlich geschieht, macht mich froh und hebt mich hinauf; denn ich empfinde, daß ich auf dem Wege bin, ein Vertrauter alles dessen zu werden, was Schönheit verkündet; . . . daß ich den Dingen immer mehr ein Jünger werde, der ihre Antworten und Geständnisse durch verständige Fragen steigert, der ihnen Weisheiten und Winke entlockt und ihre großmütige Liebe mit der Demut des Schülers leise lohnen lernt.

Und durch diese gehorsame Hingebung geht der Weg zu jener ersehnten Brüderlichkeit und Gleichheit mit den Dingen, welche wie ein gegenseitiges Beschirmen ist und vor der die letzte Angst Sage wird.[12]‡

---

* "And once more my deep soul murmurs louder,/ as if it now flowed between wider shores./ More and more the things become related to me/ and all images more and more comprehended./ I feel more intimate with the nameless one:/ With my senses, as with birds, I reach up/ from the oak tree into the windy heavens,/ and into the reflected day of the ponds,/ my feelings sink, as if standing on fishes."

† "Those are the hours when I find myself./ The meadows wave darkly in the wind,/ the bark of all the birches shimmers,/ and the evening covers them./ And I grow in rich quietude and/ would like to blossom with a hundred branches,/ in order only to bow deeply with all other things/ before the holy harmony."

‡ "And this thing which happens entirely unexpectedly, makes me happy and raises me up, for I recognize that I am on the way to becoming a confidant to all of that which

Mädchen: An Attempt at Synthesis

A further polarity in *Jugendstil* art which is closely related to the *Geist* and *Leben* theme complex, is the dichotomy between naiveté, innocence, or sexual restraint on the one hand and unsuppressed expression of sexual passion or primordial drives on the other. This polarity of emotional forces and its resultant tensions was thought by the artists of the period to be one of the basic contrasts in life, and as such became one of the fundamental elements in their works. The paradoxical figure of Salomé, whose innocent and maidenly stance is coupled with gestures of frenzied, voluptuous passion (as she was portrayed by Franz von Stuck, Aubrey Beardsley, or Gustav Klimt), represents perhaps the ultimate example.

As a poet in the *Jugendstil* mold, Rilke too allowed his works to be permeated by this same polarity. Paul Requadt attributes the poet's interest in this theme to his inherent awareness of the conflict within himself and to his exposure during the early *Jugendstil* years to the works of Richard Dehmel and Detlev von Liliencron as well as to his biased study in Munich of the early Renaissance. When Rilke eventually went to Florence, for example, and saw the art of the Renaissance with his own eyes, his intense perception of the polarity in life formed the basis of his evaluations and caused him to see in works as different as Botticelli's and Michelangelo's the same tension between passion and asceticism that he had felt in his own soul and observed in the works of his contemporaries.[13]

One of the prominent portrayals in his own writing of this polarity and its conflicts is incorporated in the figure of the cornet in the prose poem *Die Weise von Liebe und Tod des Cornet Christoph Rilke*. At the beginning of the work, the young, boyishly naive standard bearer totally immerses himself in the exciting preparations for the impending battle with the Turks. He is full of hero worship for his commander and completely caught up in the romance of the scene. At the same time, he entirely disregards the realities of the situation—the crude and lustful activities of the soldiers, the cruelty and destruction of the war, and, most importantly, the danger it represents for his own life. Furthermore,

---

represents beauty; . . . that I am becoming more and more a disciple of the things, that I increase their answers and confessions by my understanding questions, that I draw out of them wisdom and approval, and that I learn quietly to reward their generous love with my humility as their student. And through this obedient dedication, the path leads to that longed for brotherhood and equality with the things, which serves as a mutual protection and causes the ultimate fear to become a myth."

he is totally oblivious to any sensual undercurrents within himself that might otherwise have distracted his concentration on the glamorous going to war. Symbolic of his sexual innocence and naiveté is the whiteness of his uniform and the blond color of his hair which the poet repeatedly emphasizes throughout the work. The cornet has not been with the army long, however, before the other facets of his being, the underlying, passionate drives, begin to make themselves known. The first indication of this occurs as the cornet unexpectedly comes upon a naked woman who has been abused and now stands bound to a tree:

> Und er schaut: es bäumt sich. Es bäumt sich ein Leib
> den Baum entlang, und ein junges Weib,
> blutig und bloß,
> fällt ihn an: Mach mich los!
>
> Und er springt hinab in das schwarze Grün
> und durchhaut die heißen Stricke;
> und er sieht ihre Blicke glühn
> und ihre Zähne beißen.
>
> Lacht sie?
>
> Ihn graust.
> Und er sitzt schon zu Roß
> und jagt in die Nacht. Blutige Schnüre fest in der Faust.* (SW I, 240–41)

This woman, with her fiery glances and her flashing teeth, awakens in him for the first time an awareness of his erotic desires and passions. The "seething cords" which he carries off with him represent the irrepressibility of these drives and the lasting effect of the experience on the development of his life. Later, the night before the great battle, the emotions aroused by the earlier, brief encounter well up within the cornet and propel him into an overt expression of his drives and eventually to a complete awakening of the sexual passions:

EINER, der weiße Seide trägt, erkennt, daß er nicht erwachen kann; denn er ist wach und verwirrt von Wirklichkeit. So flieht er bange in den Traum und steht im Park, einsam im schwarzen Park. Und das Fest ist fern. Und das Licht lügt. Und die Nacht ist nahe um ihn und kühl. Und er fragt eine Frau, die sich zu ihm neigt:

---

* "And he peers ahead: something moves. It's a body that moves against/ the tree and a young woman,/ bloody and naked,/ pleads with him: 'Please free me!'/ And he quickly dismounts into the blackish green/ and cuts through the seething cords,/ and he sees her fiery glances/ and flashing teeth./ Is she laughing?/ He shudders./ And he is riding off on his horse already/ into the night, bloody cords held firmly in his fist."

"Bist Du die Nacht?"
Sie lächelt.
Und da schämt er sich für sein weißes Kleid.
Und möchte weit und allein und in Waffen sein.
Ganz in Waffen.

. . . .

"Frierst Du?—Hast Du Heimweh?"
Die Gräfin lächelt.
Nein. Aber das ist nur, weil das Kindsein ihm von den Schultern gefallen ist,
dieses sanfte dunkle Kleid. Wer hat es fortgenommen? "Du?" fragt er mit einer
Stimme, die er noch nicht gehört hat. "Du!"
Und nun ist nichts an ihm. Und er ist nackt wie ein
Heiliger. Hell und schlank.*   (SW I, 243–44)

He spends the night with the countess and learns the full strength and
power of his sensual drives. Before morning, there is a surprise attack
on the castle and the cornet, suddenly awakened and stunned, quickly
bids farewell to his lover and rides recklessly off into the battle and into
the middle of the advancing troops of the enemy. There he is quickly cut
down by the flashing swords. His death is as much a consequence of the
inner conflict of emotions as it is of the overpowering swords of the
Turks. Caught up once more in the early enthusiasm for battle with its
innocence and naiveté, he nevertheless cannot free himself from the
distracting memories of the past night; and in his confusion, he fails to
recognize the reality of the enemy's presence. The tension within him
produced by the onset of passion and the loss of restraint leads to his
downfall.

In a poem from the collection *Das Buch der Bilder*, the tension, without the heroic and romanticized aura of *Cornet Rilke*, again appears. "In
der Certosa" describes a monk, a member of the "white brotherhood,"
who carries out an inner, life and death struggle to attain self-control
and self-mastery over the insatiable hunger of his sexual passions:

Und seine Hände halten, wie erschlafft,
sein braunes Haupt, das schwer ist von den Säften,

* "One, wearing white satin, recognizes that he cannot awaken because he is awake and
confused by reality. Thus he flees frightened into a dream and stands in the park. Alone in
the dark park. And the festivities are far away. And the light deceives, and the night is
near to him and cool. And he asks a woman who inclines toward him: 'Are you the night?'
She smiles. And then he is ashamed of his white clothing. And he desires to be far away
and alone and ready for battle. Completely in armour. . . . 'Are you cold, are you
homesick?' The countess smiles. No. It is only because childhood has fallen from his
shoulders, this soft, dark cloak. Who has taken it from him? 'You?' he asks with a voice
which he has not yet heard. 'You!' And now there is nothing on him. And he is naked like
a saint, glowing and slender."

die ungeduldig durch das Dunkel rollen,
und sein Gewand, das faltig, voll und wollen,
zu seinen Füßen fließt, ist stramm gestrafft
um seinen Armen, die, gleich starken Schäften,
die Hände tragen, welche träumen sollen.
. . . .

Er aber sitzt, und unter den Gedanken
zerbrechen fast die breiten Handgelenke,
so schwer wird ihm der Sinn und immer schwerer.
. . . .

[Der Frate]
sinnt im Arkadenhofe der Certosa,
sinnt, wie umrauscht von rötlichen Gerüchen:
denn seine Blumen blühen alle rot.*   (SW I, 413–15)

His brown arms and head, his pulsating desires, represented by the
"juices" running through his veins, and his "red" thoughts all contrast
with his "white" robes as symbols of the intense struggle between the
forces surging within him. For the young monk, there appears to be no
relief or sublimation of the conflict.

The poem "Pietá" from the later collection *Neue Gedichte* conveys
the same conflict, and the rather startling implications of the text seem
to heighten its effect. Here, Mary Magdelena is observed caressing the
broken body of Jesus while mourning the painful passing of his life. In
her grief, she exclaims her love and passionate desire for him, and she
manifests her overwhelming frustration at his death, particularly before
their love could be fulfilled:

So seh ich, Jesus, deine Füße wieder,
die damals eines Jünglings Füße waren,
da ich sie bang entkleidete und wusch;
wie standen sie verwirrt in meinen Haaren
und wie ein weißes Wild im Dornenbusch.

So seh ich deine niegeliebten Glieder
zum erstenmal in dieser Liebesnacht.
Wir legten uns noch nie zusammen nieder,
und nun wird nur bewundert und gewacht.

---

* "And his hands hold, as if asleep,/ his brown head that is heavy with juices/ which
impatiently pulsate through the darkness,/ and his robe—folded, full, and woolen,/
flowing to his feet—is stiffly gathered/ over his arms which, like powerful shafts,/ bear the
hands which ought to be dreaming./ . . ./ But he sits, and under the thoughts/ the broad
wrists almost break,/ the meaning is so momentous to him and ever more so./ . . ./ [The
monk]/ ponders in the arcade of the certosa,/ ponders, as if surrounded by reddish smells:/
for all of his blossoms bloom red."

Doch, siehe, deine Hände sind zerrissen—:
Geliebter, nicht von mir, von meinen Bissen.
Dein Herz steht offen und man kann hinein:
das hätte dürfen nur mein Eingang sein.

Nun bist du müde, und dein müder Mund
hat keine Lust zu meinem wehen Munde—.
O Jesus, Jesus, wann war unsre Stunde?
Wie gehn wir beide wunderlich zugrund.*   (SW I, 494)

The wounds in his hands are not from her impassioned kisses, his
pierced heart is now opened to all when only she should have found a
place there, and his weary mouth no longer desires hers. The lifeless
innocence of Jesus' dead body and Mary Magdelena's frustrated, passionate outbursts form one of the most pronounced examples of the
contrast and the tension between these two forces in Rilke's works.

It is the poet's *Mädchen* (maiden) poems, however, which most
vividly portray the essence of the polarity between innocence and passion. These poems also comprise the only serious attempt in Rilke's
works to reach a fusion and lasting synthesis of these opposing forces.
As no others, the poems in question are the most closely related to the
poet's own psychological and artistic development and as such must
play an especially vital role in our discussion.

Rilke's continued and expressed sympathy with the experiences of
young girls and his deep understanding of their emotions and desires
originated undoubtedly in the crucial childhood years which he spent
dressed like a girl and living in an atmosphere dominated by women. As
he related in a letter: "Ich mußte sehr schöne Kleider tragen und ging
zur Schulzeit wie ein kleines Mädchen umher; ich glaube, meine Mutter
spielte mit mir wie mit einer großen Puppe. Im übrigen war sie immer
stolz, wenn man sie 'Fräulein' nannte. Sie wollte für jung gelten, für
leidend und für unglücklich. Und unglücklich war sie ja wohl auch. Ich
glaube, wir waren es alle."[14]† From this point until his adult years, there
was something "girlish" about him, and he found it most easy to

---

* "So, Jesus, I see your feet again/ that once were the feet of a youth/ when I apprehen-
sively bared and washed them;/ how confused they stood in my hair/ like a white bird in a
thornbush./ So I see your limbs, which were never loved,/ for the first time in this night of
love./ We never lay down together/ and now I can only admire and watch./ Yet, look, your
hands are torn,/ lover, but not by me, not by my bites,/ your heart is opened, and anyone
can enter;/ that should have been only my entry./ Now you are tired and your tired mouth/
has no more interest in my suffering mouth—./ O Jesus, Jesus, when was it our hour?/
How oddly we are both being destroyed."

† "I had to wear very pretty clothes and was dressed until school age like a girl. I believe
my mother played with me as with a large doll; otherwise, she was always proud

identify with the thoughts and feelings of *Mädchen*.[15] Implying his closeness to girls, Rilke wrote at one point:

> Mir ist, als wüßte ich so viel zu sagen
> von vielen Mädchen in den kleinen Städten,
> von sanften Bildern über ihren Betten,
> von blonden Haaren, die sie lächelnd glätten,
> von Kleidern, welche sie im Traume tragen,
> und Träumen, welche sie aus Ängsten retten,
> von kleinen Blumen auf den Fensterbretten,
> die sie sich selber zum Geburtstag gaben,
> von hundert Dingen, die sie gerne hätten,
> wenn sie schon ahnten, daß sie gerne haben.*   (SW III, 646–47)

After observing the "maidens" protrayed by *Jugendstil* artists such as Ludwig von Hofmann and Heinrich Vogeler, Rilke's initial affinities for both the girls themselves and for the art of the period were considerably reinforced. The girls' delicate features and obvious innocence mixed with just the slightest trace of curiosity about life and the earliest signs of sexual awakening reflected his personal concept of these chosen creatures. Two other artists associated with the movement in Worpswede, Paula Becker and Clara Westhoff, contributed further to Rilke's view of maidens, for he saw in them, albeit in a romanticized form, the living embodiment of these figures. For him, Becker and Westhoff were the very essence of purity and innocence, but they occasionally reflected an understanding of life which was startling in its contrast. After a visit by the two female artists in his room at Worpswede, he wrote:

Und nun sind sie hier alle so rührend in inrem Schauen. Halb Wissende, d. h. Maler, halb Unbewußte, d.h. Mädchen. Erst faßt die Stimmung sie, der ganze Ton dieser Nebelnacht mit dem fast vollen Monde über den drei Pappeln, diese Stimmung von mattem beschlagenem Silber macht sie wehrlos und zwingt sie in das Mädchensein, in das dunkle, sehnsüchtige. . . . Dann gewinnt der Künstler in ihnen Macht und schaut und schaut, und wenn er tief genug geworden ist in seinem Schauen, sind sie wieder an der Grenze ihres eigenen Wesens und Wunders und gleiten leise wieder in ihr Mädchenleben hinein.

---

whenever she was called 'Fräulein.' She wanted to be considered young, suffering, and unhappy. And unhappy she was indeed. I believe we all were."

* "It seems to me as if I knew much to tell/ about many maidens in the small cities,/ about soft pictures above their beds,/ about blond hair which smiling they smooth out,/ about clothes which they wear in a dream,/ and dreams which save them from fears,/ about small flowers in window boxes/ which they gave themselves for their birthday,/ about a hundred things which they would like to have,/ if they already realized that they like to have things."

Darum schauen sie immer lange in die Landschaft. . . . Und so standen sie an meinem Fenster . . . ¹⁶*

The exquisite atmosphere of the scene, the longing attitude of the *Mädchen* at the window, and the two facets of their personality—their maidenly innocence and their artistically aware and penetrating observation—remind us of any number of portrayals of maiden figures to be found in the works of *Jugendstil* artists. This scene underscores then not only Rilke's close personal relationship with these two maidens but also his identification of them with the art of the *Jugendstil* movement.

Besides their reinforcement of his ties with the art of the period, the two "Worpswede *Mädchen*" played an additional, vital role in Rilke's artistic development. In his many visits to their studios and in protracted artistic discussions with them during long walks through the countryside, Rilke learned of their techniques as artists and of their particular method of objective observation. In that sense they were an important source of inspiration and an impulse for artistic achievement. As "maidens," however, they were even more of an inspiration to him. They seemed to him endowed with special powers that gave him, while in their presence, an increased gift of artistic discernment and a greater ability to penetrate to the essence of life, qualities which he so earnestly sought at the time. In his diary, he wrote:

Wieviel lerne ich im Schauen dieser beiden Mädchen, besonders der blonden Malerin, die so braune schauende Augen hat! Wieviel näher fühl ich mich jetzt wieder allem Unbewußten und Wunderbaren. . . . Wieviel Geheimnisvolles ist in diesen schlanken Gestalten, wenn sie vor dem Abend stehen oder wenn sie, in samtenen Sesseln lehnend, mit allen Linien lauschen. Weil sie die Empfangensten sind, kann ich der Gebendste sein. . . . Langsam lege ich Wort für Wort auf die silberne, zarte Waage ihrer Seelen, und ich bemühe mich, aus jedem Wort ein Kleinod zu machen.¹⁷†

* "And now they are all here, so touching in their observing. Half knowing, i.e., painters, half subconscious, i.e., maidens. Now the mood catches them, the whole tone of this misty night with the almost full moon above the three poplar trees, this mood like dull, mounted silver makes them defenseless and forces them into their 'maidenness,' into the darkness, the longing. . . . Then the artist in them gains power and looks and looks, and when this artist in them has penetrated deeply enough in his observation, they arrive again at the borders of their own wonder and being and glide softly once more into their maidenly existence. For that reason, they look for a long time into the countryside. . . . And in this way, they stood at my window . . ."

† "How much I learn in observing these two maidens, especially the blond painter who has such penetrating brown eyes! How much closer I now feel to all that is subconscious and wonderful. . . . How much mystery is in these slender figures, whenever they stand in the evening and when they, resting in velvet chairs, listen with all their contours.

And in a poem, we read:

> Mädchen, Dichter sind, die von euch lernen
> das zu *sagen*, was ihr einsam *seid*;
> und sie lernen leben an euch Fernen,
> wie die Abende an großen Sternen
> sich gewöhnen an die Ewigkeit.* (SW I, 375)

As the apparent embodiment of the *Jugendstil* maidens and as a source of artistic inspiration, Paula and Clara, then, provide us with a key to an understanding of Rilke's general development in his early years as a poet as well as to a comprehension of the maiden theme.

As a result of his personal affinities and associations, Rilke preferred to portray the *Mädchen*, just as he imagined Paula and Clara to be, in a transitional stage in their development between childhood, in its fully innocent and unawakened state, and adulthood, in its erotic awareness. In some of his *Mädchen* poems, the forces of the past seem the most powerful, drawing the girls temporarily away from the future back into the innocence and inexperience of their childhood. In others, the most prevalent, a certain balance occurs between the emotions aroused by memories of the past and by the anticipation and apprehension of the future. In some few poems, Rilke even allows the erotic drives of their future life, in all its terrifying intensity, to overwhelm the girls, fully nullifying the tranquillity of their past and filling the present with great apprehension and frustration. Examples of the first type, in which childhood seems the predominant force, are found in the famous *Lieder der Mädchen*:

> Die Zeit, von der die Mütter sprachen,
> fand nicht zu unsern Schlafgemachen,
> und drin blieb alles glatt und klar.
> . . . .
>
> Wir wohnen immer tief im Turm
> und hören manchmal nur von fern
> die Wälder draußen wehn;
> und einmal blieb ein fremder Stern
> bei uns stehn.

Because they are most receptive, I am able to be so generous. . . . Slowly I place word upon word on the silvery, delicate balance of their soul, and I try to make out of each word a precious jewel."

* "Maidens, poets are those who learn from you/ to *say* that which you already *are;*/ and they learn to live from you distant ones/ just as the evenings, through large stars,/ grow accustomed to eternity."

> Und wenn wir dann im Garten sind,
> so zittern wir, daß es beginnt,
> und warten Tag um Tag—
>
> Aber nirgends ist ein Wind,
> der uns biegen mag.*   (SW I, 178)

The girls live in the isolated towers of their naiveté and perceive from a distance only the slightest breeze of erotic awakening. The erotic force seems insignificant still and really meaningless to them. They are still fully absorbed by the purity of their youth: "and therein everything remained ordered and understandable."

The *Mädchen* in the poem "Die Konfirmanden," have already abandoned their childhood and stand now at that point in their existence when life begins to make itself known to them. The day of their confirmation represents a pause in their lives precariously balanced between the past and the future. Neither realm in this brief moment seems forceful enough to take precedence over the other:

> In weißen Schleiern gehn die Konfirmanden
> tief in das neue Grün der Gärten ein.
> Sie haben ihre Kindheit überstanden,
> und was jetzt kommt, wird anders sein.
>
> O kommt es denn! Beginnt jetzt nicht die Pause,
> das Warten auf den nächsten Stundenschlag?†   (SW I, 387)

The preparations for the ceremony, the walk to the church, the church service itself, and then the long afternoon all seem interminable to the girls, and they cry out for their new life to begin: "O may it come!" Finally, the pause in their life comes to a close, and their future awakening begins softly to make itself known:

> Und draußen war ein Tag aus Blau und Grün
> mit einem Ruf von Rot an hellen Stellen.
> Der Teich entfernte sich in kleinen Wellen,

---

* "The time of which our mothers spoke/ did not find its way to our sleeping chamber./ And therein everything remained ordered and understandable./ . . ./ We still live deep in the tower/ and hear sometimes only from the distance/ the forests sighing in the wind;/ and once a star remained/ with us./ And when we are in the garden,/ we tremble that it might be beginning/ and wait day upon day—/ But nowhere is a wind/ which will bend us."

† "In white veils the confirmands/ penetrate deeply into the new green of the gardens./ They have overcome their childhood,/ and what now comes will be different./ O may it come! Does not the pause now begin,/ the waiting for the clock to strike next?"

und mit dem Winde kam ein fernes Blühn
und sang von Gärten draußen vor der Stadt.*   (SW I, 388)

The colorful impressions of the afternoon—the blue, green, and touch
of red—the distant "blossoming" whose fragrance is in the wind, and
the "singing" of the gardens outside of the city symbolically represent
the arrival of the sensual awakening.

In other works, the erotic drives are much more forceful than in the
examples above. Here, the sexual passions can no longer be denied or
suppressed, and with anxiety and even terror, the maidens attempt to
decipher the new and strange feelings welling up inside them:

Ich aber fühle, wie ich wärmer
und wärmer werde, Königin,—
und daß ich jeden Abend ärmer
und jeden Morgen müder bin.

Ich reiße an der weißen Seide,
und meine scheuen Träume schrein:
    Oh, laß mich Leid von deinem Leide,
    oh, laß uns beide
wund von demselben Wunder sein!†   (SW I, 190)

In this poem from the collection *Gebete der Mädchen zur Maria*, the young
girl feels herself being overtaken by a strange emotion which she cannot
comprehend, an emotion which both attracts and frightens her. Elsewhere, the erotic forces are even more pronounced and the maidens
lose total control of their passions in their frenzied ecstasy. Two examples from the original version of *Die weiße Fürstin* are perhaps most
extreme. At the beginning of this poetic drama, the white princess and
her younger sister Monna Lara are the very essence of maidenly purity
and virginity. As the plot develops, the princess, who, although married,
has never experienced physical love, makes elaborate plans to meet a
lover with whom she intends to escape. In anticipation of his arrival, the
two *Mädchen* fan their emotions to the point where the erotic drives take
full control. Monna Lara cries out:

Tu
mir weh.
Hack mir die Hände ins Herz.

* "And outside there was a day of blue and green/ with a touch of red in bright places./
The pond departed in small waves/ and with the wind came a distant blossoming/ which
sang about gardens outside the city."

† "I feel how I am getting warmer/ and warmer, my queen,—/ and that I am poorer every

Ich sehne mich so
nach einem Schmerz.
Oh!

Sie küssen sich.
*Pause**   (SW III, 280)

At an earlier point leading up to Monna Lara's feverish outcry, the princess unveils the emotional tension and frustration she had experienced on the first night of her marriage when her husband failed to perform his marital duty:

glühend

Ich schrie
danach. Meine bräutlichen Kissen
hab' ich mit zitternden Zähnen zerrissen,
und von dem Kreuz aus Ebenholz
schmolz
der silberne Christus los,
so groß
war die Glut
meines Brautgebets.†   (SW III, 278–79)

Despite the excesses of passages such as those in *Die weiße Fürstin*, Rilke maintained in the greatest majority of the works containing the *Mädchen* theme a tenuous balance between the impending erotic impulses and the fading of childhood tranquillity. Thus the *Mädchen* usually incorporate, as in no other Rilkean theme, a type of union of these two conflicting forces. As long as the girls existed in a transitional state, neither returning to the past nor proceeding into the future, the delicate unity of opposites could be maintained. Even in the case of the white princess who threatens more than any of Rilke's *Mädchen* to upset the balance, fate intervenes to preserve it. She is prevented at the last moment from meeting her lover by the sudden appearance of a monk of the *misericordia* and is rescued, as it were, from her primordial self. From that time on, she is constrained, we assume, to continue her maidenly existence, suspended between childlike innocence and pulsating passion.

---

evening/ and more tired every morning./ I tear at the white silk/ and my naive dreams cry out:/ O let me suffer from your suffering/ O let us both/ be wounded by the same wonder!"

* "Hurt/ me./ Hack your hands into my heart./ I long so/ for pain/ O!/ *They kiss*/ *Pause*."

† "*smoldering*/ I cried/ for it. My bridal pillows/ I tore with gnashing teeth,/ and from the cross of ebony/ the silver Christ melted,/ so great was the heat/ of my bride's prayer."

The following poem seems best to express Rilke's concept of the maidens and their "eternal" balance between the polarities of life:

> Mir sind die Mädchen immer so erschienen,
> als wohnten sie, uns fern, auf fremden Höhn
> im kühleren Frühling bei dem großen Föhn.
> Ich neige mich im Traum vor ihren Mienen;
> denn keiner weiß, wie nahe neben ihnen
> Maria geht, von einem Lächeln schön.
>
> Sie sind die Seligen, die siegend dienen,
> und also warm von Schönheit überschienen,
> daß ihre Gesten ganz in Blüten stehn.
> Und ihre tastenden Gedanken gehn
> durch die Madonnen wie durch Mandolinen.* (SW III, 646)

From their distant and immortal heights, the maidens here seem to incorporate all the ethereal qualities with which Rilke in his fantasies had endowed them. They do not belong to this world with its vulgarities and divisiveness, but, at the side of the Virgin Mary, they look down upon mere mortals, such as the poet, in order to bless and inspire.

Apparently, Rilke expected the fusion of opposites to continue in real life as well as in his poetry, at least in the "real life" as it was to be found in the idyllic "island" world at Worpswede. He hoped, it seems, that he could continue to live forever in that utopian society among artists who were "sanctified" like himself and among the *Mädchen* who were to be forever perpetuated in their transitory state. Unfortunately, these illusions could not be sustained, even in Worpswede. Things changed there too: the maidens matured, the dichotomies of life continued to clash, human concerns prevailed. In fact, at no time during his stay in the village did complete harmony reign. There were always foreign thoughts and disturbing influences present, as the events on one Sunday evening demonstrate:

Als man um Mitternacht Wein im Vogelers Keller entdeckt hatte, fragte er [Carl Hauptmann] nach einem Trinklied von mir und erklärte wiederholt, ich würde noch einmal erkennen, welche Lücke in meiner Kunst klaffte, da kein Trinklied bei mir zu finden sei. Er wollte durchaus Dehmels Trinklied singen, wovon ihm aber kein Vers einfiel. Es ist schlimm, wenn man am Ende eines Beisammenseins

---

* "To me, the maidens have always seemed/ as if they dwelled, far from us, on strange heights/ in a cooler spring with the great spring storms./ I bowed in a dream before their countenances,/ for no one knows, how close to them/ Mary walks, beautiful because of a smile./ They are the blessed ones who serve victoriously,/ and warmly illuminated by beauty/ so that their gestures stand wholly immersed in blossoms./ And their hesitating thoughts proceed/ through the Madonnas as through mandolins."

nach Wein sucht. . . . Und daß man ihn fand, machte die letzten Stunden zufallsvoll, dumm und ulkig. . . . Sonst wurde getanzt: Hauptmann mit Fräulein Westhoff. Einige Male in die Runde—Walzer . . . endlich blieb Dr. H. stehen, neigte den Kopf nachdenklich nach links, hob den Zeigefinger und konstatierte atemlos: "Jetzt fang ich an, schwindlig zu werden," womit er seiner Dame dankte. Ich war unglaublich einsam.[18]*

The ultimate blow to Rilke's illusions came suddenly in October when Paula Becker announced her engagement to Otto Modersohn, in Rilke's eyes one of the less attractive artists in the colony. This event shattered his fantasies about the maidens along with his tenuous solution to the polarities and tensions between *Geist* and *Leben* and caused in him a disappointment so strong that he had to flee Worpswede and take refuge in Berlin. After this experience, he could never again believe in the possibility of a real synthesis of these conflicting forces. Even in his writing during the later *Jugendstil* period, there is often an added tone of bitterness, regret, and recrimination in his maiden poems. The depths of his disappointment about Paula's decision comes to light much later in his requiem to her after she had suffered an untimely death in childbirth, a tragedy which confirmed in his mind his earlier feelings:

> So starbst du, wie die Frauen früher starben,
> altmodisch starbst du . . .
> den Tod der Wöchnerinnen, welche wieder
> sich schließen wollen und es nicht mehr können,
> weil jenes Dunkel, das sie mitgebaren,
> noch einmal wiederkommt und drängt und eintritt.†   (SW I, 653)

Other works indicate the same bitterness. In "Das Grabmal eines jungen Mädchens" for example, we read:

> Wir gedenkens noch. Das ist, als müßte
> alles dieses einmal wieder sein.
> Wie ein Baum an der Limonenküste

* "As at midnight wine was found in Vogeler's cellar, he [Carl Hauptmann] requested a drinking song from me and exclaimed repeatedly that I would sometime come to realize what a gap existed in my writing since I had written no drinking songs. He insisted on singing Dehmel's drinking song of which however he could not remember even one line. It is terrible when at the end of a gathering, people desire wine. . . . And that it was found made the last hours full of incidents, stupid and queer. People danced: Hauptmann with Miss Westhoff—a few times in a circle—a waltz . . . finally, Dr. H. stopped, inclined his head contemplatively to the left, raised his index finger, and stated breathlessly: 'Now I'm getting dizzy,' whereupon he thanked the lady. I was unbelievably lonely."

† "So you died as women earlier died./ Old fashioned you died . . ./ the death of women in childbirth, who again/ want to close themselves, but can no longer/ because the darkness that they also bore/ returns again and presses and enters."

trugst du deine kleinen leichten Brüste
in das Rauschen seines Bluts hinein:

—jenes Gottes.

    Und es war der schlanke
Flüchtling, der Verwöhnende der Fraun.
Süß und glühend, warm wie dein Gedanke,
überschattend deine frühe Flanke
und geneigt wie deine Augenbraun.*   (SW I, 484–85)

The young girl has been destroyed by her inner desires and by the exploitation of these desires by others. "Die Liebende" is another poem that tells of a woman crushed by the forces within her:

Ja ich sehne mich nach dir. Ich gleite
mich verlierend selbst mir aus der Hand,
ohne Hoffnung, daß ich Das bestreite,
was zu mir kommt wie aus deiner Seite
ernst und unbeirrt und unverwandt.

. . . jene Zeiten: O wie war ich Eines,
nichts was rief und nichts was mich verriet;
meine Stille war wie eines Steines,
über den der Bach sein Murmeln zieht.

Aber jetzt in diesen Frühlingswochen
hat mich etwas langsam abgebrochen
vor dem unbewußten dunkeln Jahr.
Etwas hat mein armes warmes Leben
irgendeinem in die Hand gegeben,
der nicht weiß was ich noch gestern war.†   (SW I, 377–78)

With her initial "Ja," the woman admits her desire but only begrudgingly and with hesitation. Slowly, she has lost control of herself and is without any hope of liberation: ". . . without hope of combating that/

---

* "We remember it still. It is as if/ all of this had to be again./ As a tree on the lemon coast/ you bore your small, delicate breasts/ into the rushing of his blood,/ —of that God./ And it was the slender/ refugee, the indulger of women./ Sweet and glowing, warm as your thoughts,/ overshadowing your tender flank/ and curved like your eyebrows."

† "Yes, I long for you. I glide/ slowly out of self-control/ without hope of combating that/ which comes to me as if from your side,/ serious and unerring and strange./ . . . those times: O how I was united,/ nothing that summoned and nothing that betrayed me;/ my stillness was like that of a stone,/ over which the brook murmurs./ But now, in these spring weeks,/ something slowly broke me off/ before the subconscious dark year had ended./ Something gave my poor, warm life/ into somebody's hands/ who does not know what yesterday I still was."

which comes to me as if from your side, serious and unerring and strange." The erotic force, an impersonal, strange, and unconquerable "Das," is all too persistent. She recalls the happy days of childhood when the erotic force was unknown, when nothing disturbed or betrayed her, when she, a "stone," was totally oblivious to any outside force. Now, however, her innocence, like a delicate blossom, has been broken off and discarded, and she is left to mourn its passing.

The synthesis, then, between the sensual and the ascetic, the erotic and the innocent desires had proved, at least in real life, unworkable, and the polarities of life remained as real and as problematical as ever. Rilke, like his contemporaries, discovered that he had to live with this fact, that his age and he himself were indeed full of such dichotomies. These conflicts formed a fundamental concern in his works and are one of his most consequential ties with the art of *Jugendstil*.

V. Jugendstil Structure in Rilke's Works

Scenes and Motifs

In the last chapter of this study, it shall be our task to provide the final and most conclusive evidence of the magnitude and profundity of Rilke's involvement with *Jugendstil*. Through the earlier sections dealing with the poet's critical essays and his use of themes similar to the ones of *Jugendstil*, the relationship has become evident. However, in discussing Rilke's concern with an art movement in which structure plays such a significant role and in which style demonstrates the most unique and memorable qualities, an analysis of the poet's early style and its similarities to the art of the period becomes absolutely essential. The reader will undoubtedly have perceived by now in both Rilke's essays and his poetry at least some of the tone and the spirit of *Jugendstil*, a tone which prevails in all of his writing of the period. It is now possible for us to concentrate on the specific attributes of his writing which provide this tone and spirit. On the basis of our discussion, it shall become abundantly clear that the art of *Jugendstil* furnished Rilke, in all aspects of his early works, with the primary inspiration and impetus for his creativity.

Perhaps the elemental feature of Rilke's style that points to its source in art is the pronounced tendency to imitate in verbal descriptions typical scenes from the art of *Jugendstil*. In such descriptions, the poet attempted a literal re-creation of the mood and images he had observed in the works of his artist contemporaries. Interspersed throughout his writing, as we have seen, are the characteristic decaying park landscapes, the water lilies, the swans, and the glistening reflection of the moon on water. It is of course the same quiet, isolated world of *Jugendstil* with its emotional and often mysterious atmosphere which we earlier identified as typical. One more example will suffice here:

> Wir wollen, wenn es wieder Mondnacht wird,
> die Traurigkeit zu großer Stadt vergessen
> und hingehn und uns an das Gitter pressen,
> das uns von dem versagten Garten trennt.

Wer kennt ihn jetzt . . .

. . . .

. . . allein mit seinen Blüten,
die Teiche offen, liegend ohne Schlaf.

Figuren, welche stumm im Dunkel stehn,
scheinen sich leise aufzurichten,
und steinerner und stiller sind die lichten
Gestalten an dem Eingang der Alleen.

Die Wege liegen gleich entwirrten Strähnen
nebeneinander, ruhig, eines Zieles.
Der Mond ist zu den Wiesen unterwegs;
den Blumen fließt der Duft herab wie Tränen.
Über den heimgefallenen Fontänen
stehn noch die kühlen Spuren ihres Spieles
in nächtiger Luft.*   (SW I, 167–68)

In other works, Rilke imitated the common *Jugendstil* scene of dancing maidens with their innocent, naive, yet voluptuous gestures. One
such example is the dramatic scene written for Ludwig von Hofmann,
entitled *Spiel*. Here, the author portrays a young man dressed in purple
and deep in thought who sits silhouetted against the backdrop of a
cloudless sky and an endless expanse of sea. Surrounding him is a
group of seven dancing maidens dressed in contrasting white. After an
emotional and melancholy dialogue, the maidens begin their typical
dance, which Rilke describes as follows: "Da umranken die SIEBEN
MÄDCHEN ihn ganz mit ihrem weißen Reigen. Sie neigen sich näher
über den Sinnenden, bis sie ihn endlich mit ihrem Tanz verhüllen. Auch
ihre Stimmen, die am Anfang des Gesangs hilflos und leise sind, nähern
sich, werden breiter, einiger und steigen schließlich, wie Opfersäulen
licht, in die Himmel" (SW III, 384).† The contrast of the colors symbol-
izing the basic *Jugendstil* conflict and tension between sensuality and

* "When it is a moonlit night again, we want/ to forget the sadness of large cities/ and go
up and press against the gate/ that separates us from the forbidden park./ Who recognizes
it now . . ./ . . ./ . . . alone with its blossoms,/ the opened ponds, lying there without sleep./
Figures that stand silent in the darkness/ appear to rise up softly,/ and the lustrous figures
at the entrance/ of the paths are more impenetrable and quieter./ The paths lie like
untangled strands/ beside one another, quietly, of one goal./ The moon is on its way to the
meadows;/ the fragrance flows from the flowers like tears./ Above the fountains which
have receded/ the cool traces of their game remain/ in the nightly air."

† "Then the SEVEN MAIDENS surround him entirely with their white roundelay. They
bend closer over the contemplating figure until they finally hide him with their dance.
Their voices too, which in the beginning are helpless and soft, grow closer, get broader,
more united, and finally rise, as light as pillars of burned offerings, into the heavens."

innocence and the graceful motion of the dance, which increases in intensity and emotion, point to typical scenes from von Hofmann's work and from the art of the movement at large.

In another such scene from the sketch "Kismet," the dancing maiden reminds us particularly of Franz von Stuck's and Aubrey Beardsley's Salomé with her pronounced erotic and frenzied dance:

"Was willst du?" stöhnte er.

Tjana lächelte leise: "Tanzen."

Und sie hob die schlanken, kindlich zarten Arme und ließ sie leise und langsam auf und nieder wehen, als sollten die braunen Hände Flügel werden. Sie lehnte den Kopf zurück, weit, daß die schwarzen Haare schwer hinabglitten, und schenkte ihr fremdes Lächeln dem ersten Stern. Ihre leichtgelenken bloßen Füße suchten tastend einen Rhythmus, und ein Wiegen und Schmiegen war in ihrem jungen Leib, bewußtes Genießen und willenloses Hingeben zugleich, wie es den langstieligen feinen Blumen zu eigen ist, wenn der Abend sie küßt. . . . Ein jeder Hauch, der über die Wiesen kam, schmiegte sich ihrer Bewegung in leichter, schmeichelnder Liebkosung an, und alle Blumen träumten in ihrem ersten Traum davon, sich so zu wiegen und so zu grüßen. Tjana schwebte näher und näher an den Král heran und neigte sich so fremd und seltsam, daß seine Arme gelähmt blieben vor lauter Schauen. Wie ein Sklave stand er und hörte auf das Jagen seines Herzens. Tjana wehte an ihn heran, und die Glut ihrer nahen Bewegung schlug wie eine Welle über ihn. Dann glitt sie weit, weit zurück, lächelte stolz und sieghaft und fühlte: "Er ist doch kein König" (SW IV, 54–55).*

The gesture and motions of the hands and arms of the girl, the position of her head, her flowing dark hair and strange distant smile, the erotic rhythm of her dance, and the enslaved trance of the young Král all point to the source of the sketch in *Jugendstil*.

Rilke also imitated on several occasions the typical *Jugendstil* scene where a constellation of figures, seemingly engrossed in a deep trance and surrounded by an emotionally charged atmosphere, communicate

---

* " 'What do you want?' he groaned. Tjana smiled softly: 'To dance.' And she raised her slender childlike, delicate arms and softly and slowly weaved them up and down as if her brown hands were to become wings. She leaned her head far back so that her raven hair fell down heavily and bestowed her strange smile on the nearest star. Her graceful bare feet hesitatingly sought a rhythm, and there was a rocking and a suppleness in her young body, a conscious enjoyment and at the same time an unconscious surrender like that of long-stemmed, delicate flowers whenever they are kissed by the evening. . . . Every breath that blew across the meadows nestled against her movements in light adulating caresses, and all flowers dreamed in their first dreams of rocking and greeting each other in this way. Tjana floated nearer and nearer toward Král and bent so strangely and curiously that his arms remained lame for so much watching. Like a slave he stood there and listened to the pounding of his heart. Tjana weaved toward him and the passions of her approaching motion rushed over him like waves. Then she glided far, far back, smiled proudly and victoriously and thought: 'He's really not a king.' "

with each other in exquisite silence. An example is a poem from *Buch der Bilder* entitled: "Aus einer Kindheit." Here we see a mother and her son sitting in a drawing room, the mother at the piano and the son nearby. The actual events of the poem—the arrival of the mother, her short remarks to her son, and the playing of the piano—all have very little significance by themselves. The genuine meaning is conveyed by the looks and the gestures; nothing else seems important:

> Das Dunkeln war wie Reichtum in dem Raume,
> darin der Knabe, sehr verheimlicht, saß.
> Und als die Mutter eintrat wie im Traume,
> erzitterte im stillen Schrank ein Glas.
> Sie fühlte, wie das Zimmer sie verriet,
> und küßte ihren Knaben: Bist du hier? . . .
> Dann schauten beide bang nach dem Klavier,
> denn manchen Abend hatte sie ein Lied,
> darin das Kind sich seltsam tief verfing.
>
> Er saß sehr still. Sein großes Schauen hing
> an ihrer Hand, die ganz gebeugt vom Ringe,
> als ob sie schwer in Schneewehn ginge,
> über die weißen Tasten ging.*   (SW I, 385–86)

It is particularly in his dramatic works that Rilke tended to re-create scenes from *Jugendstil*. In such scenes, as in *Spiel* quoted above, the poet inevitably had the actors stand in profile before the horizon with their hands in a meaningful gesture, their heads tilted in a manner designed to express some underlying emotion, and their eyes half-closed. Monologue and dialogue disappear at the most crucial moments since the substance of the scene is imparted to the audience by the gestures and glances of the actors, the underlying tension between the characters, and by the silence itself.

Die weiße Fürstin, already mentioned on several occasions in our study, provides the most prominent example. In the culminating scene of the play, the princess, having made plans to flee with her lover, stands alone before the horizon and awaits his arrival. From here to the end of the play, not a word more is uttered. The events which occur,

---

* "The growing darkness was like a richness in the room/ in which the boy, very secretive, sat./ And as his mother entered as if in a dream,/ a glass trembled in the silent chest./ She perceived how the room betrayed her/ and kissed her boy: 'Are you here?' . . ./ Then they both glanced anxiously at the piano,/ for many an evening she had a song/ in which the child extraordinarily immersed himself./ He sat very still. His intense glances/ hung on her hand that, totally bowed by the ring/ as if it were struggling mightily through snowdrifts,/ moved over the white keys."

their importance, and their motivation are conveyed by gesture, stance, and facial expression. The result is the re-creation of the tone and the effect of the typical *Jugendstil* work. The stage directions for the scene are as follows:

DIE WEISSE FÜRSTIN:

bleibt hoch und herrlich an der Brüstung lehnen. Sie ist stolze Erwartung und lauschende Seligkeit. Man hört: es wächst ein mutiger Rudertakt über das breite Branden des Abendmeeres hinaus. Jetzt lächelt sie: der Nachen muß nahe sein. Die weiße Fürstin langt nach dem Tuche, welches sie in weißsamtener silber-besäeter Gürteltasche
                                        trägt.

Da wird die Bewegung ungewiß erst, dann hastig, und erstarrt. Ihre Augen verirren sich im Park. Aus den Büschen tritt ihnen der Frate der Misericordia, die Maske vor dem Gesicht, entgegen und schreitet sicher und streng, den Rücken gegen das Meer, mitten in der Allee zum Schlosse hin. Schon reicht sein Schatten vor ihm an die Stufen; da
                                        wartet er.

Das Auge der weißen Fürstin hat das Meer vergessen; es reicht nichtmehr über die schwarze Gestalt des Fremden, der reglos bleibt wie sie. Und das Ruder wird wieder leiser
                    und verliert sich fern im schweren Wogenschlag.

            Die Fronte des Schlosses beginnt zu verlöschen.
            Man fühlt: die Sonne versank im Meer.

            Der Vorhang—langsam—lautlos.*   (SW III, 286–87)

Equally as imitative as the *Jugendstil* scenes and just as pronounced

* "THE WHITE PRINCESS: remains high and magnificent leaning on the ramparts. She is filled with proud expectation and the joy of listening. One hears a powerful stroke of oars above the roaring of the evening tide. Now she smiles, the boat must be near. The White Princess reaches for her handkerchief that she carries in her white satin, silver spangled purse. . Then the movement becomes first uncertain, then hurried, and finally numbed. Her eyes are diverted to the park. From the bushes steps a monk from the *misericordia* with a mask in front of his face and strides certain and sternly, his back to the sea, in the center of the path toward the castle. Already his shadow reaches out in front of him as far as the steps. There he waits. The White Princess's eyes have forgotten the sea; they are bound to the black figure of the stranger who stands as motionless as she. And the stroke of the oars gets softer again and is lost in the distance in the heavy beat of the waves. The front of the castle begins to fade. One feels: the sun has sunk into the sea. The curtain—slowly—soudlessly."

in Rilke's works are several prominent motifs which the poet obviously copied from the art of that period. These motifs, whether appearing in poems, prose pieces, or dramatic scenes, attempt to maintain the same connotative value as their counterparts in art and generally serve the function of emphasizing the all-important emotional aura of the work.

One of the most frequent of these motifs is the so-called *Teich* or pond motif which naturally appears in most of Rilke's "park" poems, but also in other contexts. Throughout his writing, this motif has a rather consistent complex of meaning which is closely related to its function in art. The *Teich* in both modes of expression most frequently signifies life itself, its depth and breadth, its past and future, its puzzlements, mysteries, and anomalies. It also represents the source of all understanding and knowledge about life; its murky depths, which cannot easily be surveyed or comprehended, reveal only rarely, in brief enlightening moments, a reflection of a basic and vital truth about life and human existence. In these moments, the figures in the works look on and discover something new and vital about their lives.

In the poem "Kindheit," for example, the persona of the poem bends over the surface of the pond while recollecting various experiences of his childhood—the frenzied games, the apprehensions, and the feelings of inferiority. During his reminiscences, he seems to catch a glimpse in the pond of his face as a child, which then slowly fades away. For a brief moment, his childhood has come to life again, and although the face recedes once more into the murky waters, a part of his existence has been revealed to him. Unfortunately, he cannot conjure up the vision again since he has no control over these revelations, and he must continue to ponder the full significance of his lost youth:

> Und stundenlang am großen grauen Teiche
> mit einem kleinen Segelschiff zu Knien;
> . . . .
> und denken müssen an das kleine bleiche
> Gesicht, das sinkend aus dem Teiche schien—:
> O Kindheit, o entgleitende Vergleiche.
> Wohin? Wohin?*   (SW I, 385)

That the *Teich* represents the source of all knowledge and understanding about existence becomes abundantly clear in a poem from "Die Bilder entlang," written for Ludwig von Hofmann. In this poem, the

---

* "And for hours kneeling at the great, grey pond/ with a small sailboat;/ . . ./ and having to think of the small, pale/ face that sinking appeared from the pond—:/ O childhood, O fading comparisons./ Whereto? Whereto?"

young girls, again portrayed in a transitional period of their lives, begin the process of learning about adulthood with a symbolic "looking into the pond":

> Wir waren dunkel an dem Saum der Sonnen
> und ohne Traum und ohne Anvertrauen;
> und jede Furcht und jedes Fest der Frauen
> hat erst begonnen
> mit unserem ersten In-die-Teiche-Schauen.*   (SW III, 623)

Another poem, entitled "Fortschritt," in which the poet feels a resurgence of life's forces within himself, portrays metaphorically his increased artistic perception as a submergence into the *Teich*. Here the poet finds communion with life and understanding of its meaning:

> Und wieder rauscht mein tiefes Leben lauter,
> als ob es jetzt in breitern Ufern ginge.
> . . . .
> und in den abgebrochnen Tag der Teiche
> sinkt, wie auf Fischen stehend, mein Gefühl.†   (SW I, 402)

The *Teiche* in this poem are usually "abgebrochen," that is, non-reflective, non-revealing, uncommunicative; but, as the poet penetrates figuratively below the surface and proceeds to the depths, the ponds begin to give up their secrets.

As a variation on the motif of the *Teich*, Rilke creates, at other times in his writing, descriptions of certain sacrosanct *Jugendstil* figures— women, peacocks, or swans—in connection with the ponds. In these descriptions, the poet seems to indicate the harmony and unity of these special figures with the source of life. In one poem, he writes for example:

> Ich will durch lange Hallen schleichen
> und in die tiefen Gärten schauen,
> die über alle Marken reichen.
> Und Frauen lächeln an den Teichen
> und in den Wiesen prahlen Pfaun . . .‡   (SW I, 112)

---

* "We were dark at the borders of the sun/ and without a dream and without trust;/ and every anxiety and each celebration of women/ began only/ with our first looking into the pond."

† "And once more my deep soul murmurs louder,/ as if it now flowed between wider shores./ . . ./ and into the reflected day of the ponds,/ my feelings sink, as if standing on fishes."

‡ "I desire to creep through long halls/ and look into the deep gardens/ that reach beyond all borders./ And women smile beside the ponds,/ and in the meadows peacocks strut . . ."

In a poem from *Lieder der Mädchen*, Rilke associates the quiet anticipation of maidens with vessels moored at the bank of a pond; in a moment of release, they transform into swans:

> Ihr Mädchen seid wie die Kähne;
> an die Ufer der Stunden
> seid ihr immer gebunden,—
> darum bleibt ihr so bleich;
> ohne hinzudenken,
> wollt ihr den Winden euch schenken:
> euer Traum ist der Teich.
> Manchmal nimmt euch der Strandwind
> mit bis die Ketten gespannt sind
> und dann liebt ihr ihn:
> > Schwestern, jetzt sind wir Schwäne,
> > die am Goldgesträhne
> > die Märchenmuschel ziehn.*   (SW I, 175)

The poet himself longs to be like the pond that encompasses the essence of life, the true reality:

> Solchen stillen Bildern will ich gleichen
> und gelassen aus den Rosen reichen
> welche widerkommen und vergehn;
> immerzu wie einer von den Teichen
> dunkle Spiegel immergrüner Eichen
> in mir halten, und die großen Zeichen
> ungezählter Nächte näher sehn.†   (SW I, 163)

In all of Rilke's works, the pond is inseparably connected with the search for the essence of life, and thus the poetic motif virtually coincides in meaning with the identical image to be found in *Jugendstil* painting.

If judged by its frequency, the *Hand* motif seems equally as common and as important to Rilke in his *Jugendstil* writing as the *Teich* motif. Often because of an exaggerated or peculiar gesture, these hands, throughout the art of this period, take on a particularly expressive quality and, as a result, become the single most significant element in the portrayal of

---

* "You maidens are like the boats;/ you are always tied/ to the shore of hours,—/ thus you remain so pale;/ without reflection,/ you want to give yourselves to the winds:/ your dream is the pond./ Sometimes the wind at the shore takes you with it/ till the chains are taut/ and then you love the wind:/ Sisters, now we are swans/ who in the golden harness/ pull the fairy-tale shell."

† "I want to be like such still pictures/ and calmly reach forth from the flowers/ that come again and wilt;/ always hold inside me, like one of the ponds,/ dark mirrors of always green oaks,/ and see more clearly the great signs/ of innumerable nights."

underlying meaning (cf. illus. 5). Rilke's use of this motif corresponds exactly to that of the other arts in that his "hands" also assume the essential connotative role in the work. Rilke was especially fond of combining this motif with the *Mädchen* theme, where the hands serve the function of expressing the delicate and precarious position of the maidens on the brink of adulthood. The hands portray here both the longing for sexual fulfillment and the fear and apprehension of the future.

In the *Lieder der Mädchen*, many examples of such expressive hands appear. At one point the maidens stand at dusk surrounded by the sensual fragrance of blossoms and wonder about their future:

> Der Abend wird den Blüten schwer,
> die Schwestern stehn in Scham
> und halten ihre Hände her
> und lauschen lang und lächeln leer,—
> und eine jede sehnt sich: wer
> ist unser Bräutigam . . . *   (SW I, 175)

The gesture of holding forth the hands, as in a painted scene, conveys the entire range of emotional nuances of the situation: desire, sensual awakening, but also uncertainty and fear. In another poem, the *Mädchen* are particularly apprehensive about the future, and again, it is the hands that express this emotion clearly to the reader:

> Eh der Garten ganz beginnt
> sich der Güte hinzugeben,
> stehn die Mädchen drin und beben
> vor dem zögernden Erleben,
> und aus engen Ängsten heben
> sie die Hände in den Wind.†   (SW I, 176)

They raise their hands into the wind as a sign of their attempt to throw off the overwhelming fear which has befallen them. In a poem from *Gebete der Mädchen zur Maria*, the hands convey the fatigue and lifelessness of the maidens' mothers who have been worn down by the drudgery of their existence:

> Unsre Mütter sind schon müd;
> und wenn wir sie ängstlich drängen,

* "The evening gets heavy for the blossoms,/ the sisters stand in shame/ and hold forth their hands/ and listen intently with empty smiles,/ and each one longs to know:/ 'Who is our bridegroom . . .'"

† "Before the garden begins completely/ to succumb to its fullness,/ the maidens stand in it and tremble/ before the halting experience/ and from narrow anxieties they/ raise their hands into the wind."

> lassen sie die Hände hängen,
> und sie glauben fernen Klängen:
>> Oh, wir haben auch geblüht!*   (SW I, 184)

The girls' hands, in contrast, are young, full of life, and convey the rising passion from within: "und da sehn sie unsre heißen/ Hände nicht . . ." (SW I, 184–85: "and then they don't see/ our hot hands").

The young monk of "In der Certosa," whose plight resembles, as we have seen earlier,[1] the dilemma of the maidens, expresses the emotional tension within him by the position of his hands. His broad wrists are equally as strained by the surging emotions as the maidens' more delicate ones. The hands continue in many more poems to represent the emotional state and the fate of the maidens. Their hands blossom, for example, like delicate flowers:

> . . . Aus deines Kleides Seidensaum
> blühn deine weißen Mädchenhände
> wie Lilien im Mainachttraum.†   (SW III, 446)

They also become easily tired and weak:

> Und auf den rauschenden Etüden
> trieb ihre Seele leis davon.
> Sie sah ihr nach. Und ihre Müden
> Cäcilienhände schliefen schon.‡   (SW III, 579)

On occasion, the hands represent the suffering of the frail *Mädchen* as they are forced to be subservient to others. In these instances, as in the case of the mothers' hands referred to above, the maidens' hands threaten to become worn out and lifeless:

> Du, Hände, welche immer geben,
> die müssen blühn von fremden Glück.
> . . . Das sind die Hände mit den schmalen
> Gelenken, die sich leise mühn.§   (SW I, 125–26)

Other Rilkean motifs, closely associated with the *Geist* and *Leben* and the *Mädchen* themes and modeled on the visual effects of the art of

---

* "Our mothers are already tired;/ and if we anxiously pressure them,/ they let their hands hang,/ and they believe distant sounds:/ O, we also blossomed!"

† "From the silken border of your dress/ your white maiden's hands blossom/ like lilies in a dream in a night in May."

‡ "And upon the rushing études/ her soul softly fled./ She watched it go. And her tired/ Cecilia hands slept already."

§ "You hands, which always give,/ they must blossom from the happiness of others./ . . . These are the hands with the small/ wrists that softly struggle."

5. *Ferdinand Hodler: "Spring" (Museum Folkwang, Essen)*

Jugendstil, are the color groups of red and white. These colors, although utilized by Rilke consistently and profusely much earlier than Worps-wede, assumed like Heinrich Vogeler's colors an independent and spe-cific symbolic or connotative value all their own, and whenever they appear in his writings express one or the other aspect of the emotional polarity inherent in the themes mentioned above.[2] The white group which includes various shades of white as well as blond, and sometimes silver, invariably implies the purity, innocence and naiveté of the figures or, on occasion, their sense of weariness with life. The red group, including red, purple, brown, and sometimes colors such as dark green, symbolizes the instinctual, vitalistic side of existence. When a girl's hand is white, her hair blond, or her complexion pale, we become aware of her withdrawn emotional state; likewise, if her clothing is purple or her arms brown, we focus on the surging impulses within her. These color motifs often occur by themselves or appear in juxtaposition to one another to create the typical *Jugendstil* tension; their connotation, how-ever, is always the same.

In passage after passage throughout Rilke's works of the period, we may discover examples such as: "Ein Mädchen, weiß und vor der Abendstunde . . ." (SW III, 697: "A maiden, white and standing before the twilight hour . . ."); "In weißen Schleiern gehen die Konfirmanden" (SW I, 387: "In white veils the confirmands walk"); or, "Einer, der weiße Seide trägt . . ." (SW I, 243: "One who wears white satin . . ."). By reference to the color white, all of these phrases emphasize the inno-cence and purity of the figures portrayed. In contrast to the white of innocence, the group of red colors evoke a radically different emotional state: "Wir langen alle ungelenk/ den roten Rosen nach" (SW I, 183: "We all reach out awkwardly/ for the red roses"); "Keine braunen Mädchen, die sich samten/ breiteten in Tropenmüdigkeit;/ keine Augen, die wie Waffen flammten . . ." (SW I, 394: "No brown maidens who relaxed velvety/ in tropic weariness;/ no eyes which flamed like weap-ons . . ."); or, "Und sie hob die schlanken, kindlich zarten Arme . . . als sollten die braunen Hände Flügel werden" (SW IV, 54: "And she raised her slender childlike, delicate arms . . . as if her brown hands were to become wings"). In each instance, the crucial word is a modifier ex-pressing color that conveys the sentiment of the moment.

Rilke also creates entire episodes in his works in which these color motifs play a fundamental and expressive role. In the poem "In der Certosa," quoted above, the young monk, dressed in the austere white robes of his order, nevertheless seems about to succumb to the primor-dial urges welling up within him. The tension between his vows and his emotional drives is epitomized by the contrast of the two groups of colors. On the one hand, his white cloak that is "stramm gestrafft" (stiffly gathered) serves as a symbol of his strict and inflexible vows. Contrasted with the cloak are his hands and his head: "Und seine Hände halten, wie erschlafft,/ sein braunes Haupt, das schwer ist von den Säften. . . ." ("And his hands hold, as if asleep, his brown head that is heavy with juices . . ."). Finally, he seems completely surrounded by "rötliche Gerüche" ("reddish scents") and even the flowers in his garden plot blossom forth in red: "denn seine Blumen blühen alle rot" ("for all of his blossoms bloom red") (SW I, 413–15). The same color contrasts prevail in the tension surrounding the figure of the Cornet in *Cornet Rilke* and the White Princess in *Die weiße Fürstin*. One final and rather vivid example of such an episode and of such color contrasts occurs in the early collection *Traumgekrönt*:

> Du warst von unserm weiten Weg erschlafft,
> ich sagte leise deinen süßen Namen:
> Da bohrte sich mit wonnewilder Kraft
> aus deines Herzens weißem Liliensamen
> die Feuerlilie der Leidenschaft.
>
> Rot war der Abend—und dein Mund so rot,
> wie meine Lippen sehnsuchtheiß ihn fanden,
> und jene Flamme, die uns jäh durchloht,
> sie leckte an den neidischen Gewanden . . . *   (SW I, 93–94)

A further motif, the so-called *Falten* (folds) motif, demonstrates perhaps more than any other Rilke's dependence on the visual arts of *Jugendstil* as a model. In the art of the period, the artists often relied on expressive folds in the clothing worn by the main figures to lend an emotional aura to their works. These folds seemed to assume the inner emotions of the figures and to convey them visually to the audience. The fact that Rilke adopted in his own works the visual image of the folds and abandoned more detailed literary descriptions, testifies to his strong reliance on the art of the *Jugendstil* movement. In his writing, these *Falten* also reinforce the emotional aura of the individual figures and occasionally even of the entire work. In order to accomplish this effect, the folds often are personified so that they react as the figures themselves do to their surroundings, thus reflecting and visualizing the inner feelings.

---

* "You had fallen asleep because of the long way;/ I spoke softly your sweet name:/ then with rapturously wild power/ the firelily of passion erupted/ from the lily white embryo of your heart./ The evening was red, and your mouth so red/ as my lips, hot with longing, discovered it,/ and that flame which rapidly consumed us/ licked at the envious raiment . . ."

An example of the motif in question can be found in a passage from *Cornet Rilke*. During the ball on the night preceding the great battle, the young flag bearer is dazzled by the great splendor of the hall and by the stunning beauty of the women. Not only do their facial expressions and the gestures of their hands convey to him their inner being but the folds of their gowns do so just as vividly:

Denn nur im Schlafe schaut man solchen Staat und solche Feste und solche Frauen. Ihre kleinste Geste ist eine Falte, fallend in Brokat. Sie bauen ein Lachen auf aus silbernen Gesprächen und manchmal heben sie die Hände so, und du mußt meinen, daß sie irgendwo hoch in den Lüften blasse Rosen brächen, die du nicht siehst. Und da willst du geschmückt sein mit ihnen . . . (SW III, 299).*

In "Die Konfirmanden," the folds of the clothing again depict the underlying emotions of the young girls. The dresses now have changed from the heavy and "passionate" brocade of the women of the court to the white and "innocent" confirmation dresses. Although the maidens are still naive and sexually unawakened, the folds of their white dresses reveal a soft reflection of colors, signifying the imminent advent of adult life:

Und es war still, als der Gesang begann:
Wie Wolken stieg er in der Wölbung an
und wurde hell im Niederfall; und linder
denn Regen fiel er in die weißen Kinder.
Und wie im Wind bewegte sich ihr Weiß,
und wurde leise bunt in seinen Falten
und schien verborgne Blumen zu enthalten . . .†   (SW I, 387)

The White Princess conveys to us her innocence, her melancholia, and also her erotic desires by the folds of her gown:

DIE WEISSE FÜRSTIN:
Lehnt vorn auf der Steinbank. Sie trägt ein weiches, weißes Gewand mit müden, willigen Falten. In ihren Augen
        ist ein Warten und Lauschen.‡   (SW III, 268)

* "For only in dreams does one see such finery and such banquets and such women. Their smallest gesture is a fold falling in brocade. They form a laughter from silver conversations, and occasionally they raise their hands in such a way that you have to think that they are picking pale roses that you can't see, somewhere high in the air. And you want to be adorned with them . . ."

† "And it was quiet as the song began./ Like clouds it rose in the dome/ and became bright as it fell again to earth; and gentler/ than rain, it fell on the white children./ And their whiteness moved as if in the wind,/ and became softly colored in its folds/ and appeared to contain hidden flowers . . ."

‡ "THE WHITE PRINCESS:/ Leans forward on the stone bench. She wears a soft,/ white gown with tired, willing folds. In her eyes there/ is a waiting and a listening."

And the angels who appear to the shepherds in "Verkündigung über den Hirten" demonstrate the importance of their task and their personal majesty by the folds of their heavenly robes:

> Und die Hirten waren aufgestanden,
> und die dunklen Herden schwankten schwer,—
> und die Engel kamen hinterher,
> wachsend und in faltigen Gewanden . . . *   (SW III, 699)

This poem, it should be noted, was written directly under the inspiration of Vogeler's painting "Die Verkündigung" in which the angel's robes perform the same expressive function.

A final, particularly pronounced example of the *Falten* motif in Rilke's works is the poem "Bildnis aus der Renaissance," written in 1899:

> Ihre Seele stieg in ihr entflammtes
> Aug, wie in die Rüstung steigt der Wächter
> weißer Türme oder sanfter Frauen
> (eh die Blicke noch den Feind erschauen,
> in der ersten Ahnung seines Amtes),
> und sie hebt mit ihrem Atmen breit
> in den Glanz ihr schweres Halsgeschmeid;
> und in ihrem rotverloschnen Kleide
> ist ein Kämpfen zwischen Samt und Seide
> und ein dunkler Widerstreit:
> bis der Falten seidenes Gelächter
> abbricht an dem Rand des ernsten Samtes.†   (SW III, 640)

Obviously inspired by a painting from the Renaissance, this poem depicts "visually" the passionate inner turmoil of the woman by the struggle between the silken and velvet folds of her gown, a struggle which ultimately results in a victory for the sensuous and exquisite velvet (the woman's primordial drives) over the cynical silk (her conscious intellect).

Lastly, Rilke adopted one of the basic structural elements of *Jugendstil*, the energized, undulating line, to create the *Wellen* (wave) motif. In a typical art work from the period, as we have seen, these lines distin-

---

* "And the shepherds got up/ and the dark herds swayed heavy,/ and the angels came afterwards,/ growing and with folds in their raiment."

† "Her soul rose in her impassioned/ eyes like a guard of white towers or of soft women/ climbs to the fortifications/ (before his eyes catch sight of the enemy,/ in the first intimation of his responsibilities),/ and she raises broadly into the light her heavy/ necklace with her breathing;/ and in her red extinguished gown/ there is a struggle between velvet and silk/ and a dark retaliation,/ until the folds of silken laughter/ break off at the border of the stern velvet."

guish the various elements from one another with a bold outline while at the same time uniting them into a harmonized whole. The pulsations of the lines also seem to enliven and energize the work. As a motif in Rilke's writing, however, the lines or waves lose this basic function and become, as part of the description, a reinforcement of the precious, exquisite, and decorative tone of his style. Thus, by changing the undulating waves from a structural element to a connotative one, Rilke has also changed their role and meaning.

Rilke's waves project in several poems, for example, the emotional aura of the work. In one poem, the poet's own reaction to a maiden is conveyed by the contours of her silhouette as she stands before the horizon:

> Ein Mädchen, weiß und vor der Abendstunde . . .
> und immer wieder fühl ich sie wie Funde:
> nicht nur sie selbst sind mir so wunderbar;
> die leisen Linien von Hals und Haar,
> und wie sie grenzen vor dem Hintergrunde.
>
> Sie leben lange in Konturen nur.
> Und auch die Worte, die sie abends haben,
> vor Wiesenblumen oder Waisenknaben,—
> sind ganz Kontur . . . *   (SW III, 697)

The maiden here is particularly dazzling because of her wonderful "lines"; even her words take on strong "contours." In the poem "Zierstück," we discover not only the meaningful folds of clothing of the maiden but also the trembling lines of *Jugendstil* which together express the maiden's emotional state:

> Aus deinem Haar,
> aus des Gewandes Falten,
> aus deinem Gang
> fühl ich deinen verhallten
> Gesang,
> Mädchen, und weiß, wie er war.
>
> Einsam hast du gesungen,—
> man siehts.

* "A maiden, white and standing before the evening hour . . ./ and again and again I perceive them as a treasure:/ They themselves not only are so wonderful, but also/ the soft lines from their neck and hair,/ and how they give outline before the background./ They exist for a long time only in contours./ And also the words that they speak in the evenings/ before wild flowers or orphan boys/ are wholly contour . . ."

Alle Linien deines jungen
Leibes zittern, halbbezwungen
von der Liebe des Lieds.*   (SW III, 626)

From the maiden's hair, the folds of her clothes, her walk, and especially
the quivering contours of her body, the perceptive persona of the poem
discerns her inner, erotic struggle. In another example, a poem in which
the poet again feels an awakening of the forces of life within him, the
waves indicate the expansion of his soul as it begins to transcend the
limitation of the common world. Finally, it unites with the universe
through the pulsating "waves of infinity":

Da wächst die Seele mir, bis sie in Scherben
den Alltag sprengt; sie wird so wunderweit:
An ihren morgenroten Molen sterben
die ersten Wellen der Unendlichkeit.†   (SW I, 125)

The lines or waves in other works are described as the unifying
force between the various figures in the poem and their surroundings.
In one example, the figures stand trembling before the statue of Venus
while the silent waves of emotion surround them and unite them with
each other and the park:

Sie treten in den späten Park und stellen
sich um das Bad der weißen Venus, die
so gerne, zögernd auf den Marmorschwellen,
in alle schreckenden Geräusche schrie.
Sie stellen sich wie eine Melodie:
die Schattigen, die Blassen und die Hellen.
Und heitres Schweigen geht in breiten Wellen
wie in Gesprächen über sie . . .‡   (SW III, 650)

In several poems, the *Wellen* attempt to unite lovers in an emotional
communion, a communion which for Rilke too is fraught with severe
difficulties. The undulating waves in these cases often emanate from the

* "From your hair/ from the folds of your cloak/ from your step/ I feel your restrained/
song,/ maiden, and know, how it was. ./ You have sung alone,—/ one notices it./ All the
lines of your young body/ tremble, half-subdued,/ from the love of the song."

† "My soul grows until it bursts into splinters/ the ordinary day. It becomes so wonder-
fully wide./ On its sunrise pier,/ the first waves of infinity break."

‡ "They enter into the late park and place/ themselves around the fountain of the White
Venus/ who, hesitating on the marble edge,/ would like so much to cry out to all the
startling sounds./ They place themselves like a melody:/ the shadowy ones, the pale ones,
and the bright ones./ And a happy silence washes over them/ in broad waves as in
conversation . . ."

slightest physical movement of the figures or even from their thoughts and pervade the space separating them. In the poem "Die Stille," the waves are transmitted, but unfortunately one partner cannot or does not choose to receive them, and there is no reciprocation:

> Hörst du, Geliebte, ich hebe die Hände—
> hörst du: es rauscht . . .
> . . . .
> Der Abdruck meiner kleinsten Bewegung
> bleibt in der seidenen Stille sichtbar;
> unvernichtbar drückt die geringste Erregung
> in den gespannten Vorhang der Ferne sich ein.
> . . . .
> Nur die ich denke: Dich
> seh ich nicht.*   (SW I, 379)

In another poem from *Neue Gedichte*, a lover laments the fact that he cannot free himself from the tyrannical communion of souls and that he must respond to these waves of communication whenever they are transmitted by his partner:

> Wie soll ich meine Seele halten, daß
> sie nicht an deine rührt? Wie soll ich sie
> hinheben über dich zu andern Dingen?
> Ach gerne möcht ich sie bei irgendwas
> Verlorenem im Dunkel unterbringen
> an einer fremden stillen Stelle, die
> nicht weiterschwingt, wenn deine Tiefen schwingen.†   (SW I, 482)

In all of the above, Rilke obviously copied artistic effects he had observed in various works of *Jugendstil*. But a description of a phenomenon does not create the same effects as the phenomenon itself. In the above examples, the waves assume a purely connotative role and as such appear rather affected and superficial. In order to enliven his works in the same manner as he observed in the works of *Jugendstil*, the poet had to arrive at other means more indigenous to his own medium.

---

* "Do you hear, lover, I raise my hands—/ do you hear, it murmurs . . ./ . . ./ The impression of my smallest movement/ remains visible in the silky stillness;/ indestructible the tiniest motion/ imprinted on the tense curtain of the distance./ . . ./ Only the one about whom I am thinking—you,/ I do not see."

† "How shall I prevent my soul from/ touching yours? How shall I raise it/ up and beyond you to other things?/ O how gladly I would like to find it/ shelter with something that is lost in the darkness/ in a strange, quiet place that does/ not respond whenever your depths pulsate."

Structural Adaptations

Rilke was not content merely to imitate various scenes, motifs, and compositional elements of *Jugendstil* in his writing; he also sought to recreate certain of the movement's fundamental stylistic characteristics in the very structure of his own medium of expression.[3] With these stylistic transformations the poet attempted to produce the same effects he discovered in the painting and sculpture of *Jugendstil*, and in this context the full extent of the influence of the visual arts on his creativity can be shown. When *Jugendstil* structures become an essential component of Rilke's work, his writing demonstrates a high level of artistry and individuality. It is our purpose in the concluding section of this work to investigate these literary adaptations in order finally to provide the most important element in our overall view of Rilke and his relationship with *Jugendstil*.

Initially, it is necessary to mention once more two of the important traits prevalent in the art of the movement. The first is the artist's primary emphasis on style or the manner of his presentation and his only secondary concern with the content or theme. Thus in a typical work from the period, the costly and decorative materials, the composition, and the particular constellation of the various figures or elements all play a more important role than the actual subject itself. Heinrich Vogeler's sketches are unique, in reality, less for their fairy tale or mythological themes than for the manner of their conception and execution. The ornamental qualities, the materials, and the atmosphere all are endowed with special value aside from the theme and exist independently of the content.

The second trait is an extension of the first. As we have seen, the essential meaning of the work, throughout the art of the period, is the underlying, emotional one (Dolf Sternberger called it that "atmosphere of the soul")[4] which relies to great extent on the decorative style for expression and materialization. Thus the style also plays an essential role in conveying the emotional tone or aura of the work.

Rilke's literary works demonstrate the same perspective and emphasis, the same primary concern with style and underlying tone. In his writing, there had always existed from his earliest poems a tendency toward the decorative and the unusual. H. W. Belmore called him, for example, the "born rhymster . . ."[5] This tendency was only intensified by his exposure to the art of the period, with its emphasis on the independent and ornate qualities of style. The poet's increased use of decorative elements as he emphasized style became one of his initial adaptations of *Jugendstil* to his own works.

Like his contemporaries, Rilke often utilized in his writing elements which had no intrinsic thematic justification, elements which existed for their own sake and because the author took delight in them. There is no other basis for the poet's profuse use of inner rhyme, alliteration, assonance, and other such devices. In their use, the poet endows his works with much of the same stylistic mannerism that pervades the *Jugendstil*:

> In leiser Luft die Ranken schwanken,
> wie wenn wer Abschied winkt.—Am Pfad
> stehn alle Rosen in Gedanken;
> sie sehen ihren Sommer kranken
> und seine hellen Hände sanken
> leise von seiner reifen Tat.*   (SW III, 238)

The examples here of alliteration, such as "leiser Luft," "wie wenn wer . . . winkt," and "sie sehen . . . Sommer," and of inner rhymes, e.g., "Ranken schwanken," are literary equivalents of the typically decorative *Jugendstil* work. Added to these elements of rhyme and alliteration are the repeated inclusion of assonance in the poems and the creation of new compounds or even new words altogether:

> Das sind die Gärten, an die ich glaube:
> Wenn das Blühn in den Beeten bleicht,
> und im Kies unterm löschenden Laube
> lindenleuchtendes Schwiegen schleicht.†   (SW III, 222)

The similarity of sounds in words such as "Schweigen schleicht" and "lindenleuchten" point to Rilke's experimentation with language to create the most decorative qualities possible. The same is true of the following:

> Zart wie ein zages Birkenbeben
> bleibt von dem gebenden Erleben
> ein Rhythmenzittern drin zurück.‡   (SW I, 125)

The word compounds "Birkenbeben" and "Rhythmenzittern" probably

---

* "In the quiet air, the vines weave back and forth,/ as if someone waved goodbye.—In the path/ all the roses stand in thought;/ they see their summer growing ill/ and its lustrous hands sank/ softly because of its consummate deed."

† "Those are the gardens in which I believe:/ when the blooms fade in the flower beds,/ and on the gravel under waning foliage/ the silence like the shining of linden trees creeps."

‡ "Delicate like the timid quivering of birches,/ a trembling of rhythms from the revealing experience/ remains behind in it."

occur nowhere else but in these poems and have been created obviously for their ornamental effect.

A more fundamental adaptation of the *Jugendstil* emphasis on style, however, is Rilke's alteration of the traditional syntactic structure of sentences. Though the subject and verb normally form the axis of a sentence and convey to the reader the most important elements of understanding, namely the actor and the action, Rilke, in his *Jugendstil* works, placed the primary importance on the modifiers—adverbs, adjectives, and modifying phrases—so that the manner in which the event occurs assumes more prominence in our minds than the event itself. The modifiers form the new axis of the sentence, and the subject and verb become almost incidental, serving basically grammatical functions. Thus the style becomes more vital than the content, and the "atmosphere of the soul" more clearly enunciated.

Rilke altered the syntactic emphasis of his sentences by a variety of means. He purposefully weakened the action by his choice of intransitive, reflexive, or the copulative verbs *sein* (to be) and *werden* (to become). He then surrounded and overwhelmed these verbs with a myriad of adverbs and adverbial phrases. He likewise diminished the importance of the subject by obscuring it also in a super-abundance of adjectival modifiers, appositives, and relative clauses. In a typical sentence from a poem of the period, the usual intransitive verb, the neglected subject, and the all-important phrases and clauses are evident: "Und wenn von Hügeln, die sich purpurn saümen,/ in bleiche Bläue schwimmt der Silberkahn,—/ dann unter schattenschweren Blütenbäumen/ seh ich es [das Glück] nahn" (SW I, 95).* In the first clause, the verb "schwimmen" serves only the grammatical function of uniting the subject with the predicate and is entirely over-shadowed by what precedes and follows it. The subject, "Silberkahn" (silver boat), although more noticeable by virtue of its color context, is almost forgotten too in the series of phrases and clauses. The transitive verb in the second half of the sentence, although more forceful than "schwimmen," is also weakened by the addition of the infinitive "nahn" (nearing) and by the phrases which precede it. The subject, "ich" (I), plays virtually no role whatsoever. The really essential elements—"Und wenn von Hügeln" ("And when from hills"), "die sich purpurn säumen" ("that are hemmed in purple"), and "unter schattenschweren Blütenbäumen" ("under heavy-shadowed, blossoming trees")—remain foremost in our minds. The inverted word order itself further emphasizes the stress on the modifying

* "And when from hills that are hemmed in purple/ in pale blueness the silver boat proceeds—/ then under heavy-shadowed, blossoming trees/ I see it nearing."

phrases and clauses. An additional example from *Cornet Rilke* demonstrates the same stylistic proclivities: "Aus dunklem Wein und roten Rosen rinnt die Stunde rauschend in den Traum der Nacht" (SW III, 299: "From dark wine and red roses the hour flows rustling into the dream of the night"). The phrases "Aus dunklem Wein und roten Rosen" ("from dark wine and red roses") and "in den Traum der Nacht" ("into the dream of the night") receive far more prominence than the subject "Stunde" (hour). The adverb "rauschend" (rustling), the typical present participle modifier, alters the action of the sentence by diverting our attention away from the verb toward itself.

Rilke's choice of modifiers further stresses the style and heightens the emotional tone of the work. He demonstrates a clear preference for words which create a rarified and exquisite tone. The objects or figures in his works are "zart" (delicate), "sanft" (soft), "still" (still), or "seiden" (silken). They react to their surroundings with "Zittern" (trembling), "Rauschen" (rushing), or "Schauern" (quivering). They possess attributes which are "glänzend" (shining) or "schimmernd" (schimmering) or "samten" (velvety). The poet, as the following examples illustrate, tends also to utilize comparatives or superlatives for their own sake rather than to suggest a real comparison, thereby magnifying the emotional aura of the work: "Und sie kniete knieender, die Hände/ fester faltend, daß er sie bestände" (SW I, 618: "And she kneeled more 'kneelingly,' the hands/ folded more firmly that he might withstand her"); "Vom goldensten Ringe/ ließ ich dein Feuer umfassen,/ und er müßte mirs halten/ über die weißeste Hand" (SW I, 265: "By the most golden ring,/ I had your fire captured,/ and it had to contain it for me/ on the whitest hand"); "Und der schwarze Pfad wird leiser,/ fernes Ave weht die Luft—" (SW I, 116: "And the black path gets softer/ distant aves wave through the air"); "O wie blüht mein Leib aus jeder Ader/ duftender, . . . ich gehe schlanker und gerader,/ und du wartest nur—" (SW I, 485: "O how my body blossoms from every vein/ more fragrant . . . I walk more slender and straighter,/ and you wait only . . .").

Rilke also used throughout his writing of the period a type of color lyricism to strengthen the emotional aura of his work. These color modifiers, in contrast to the color motifs mentioned earlier, possess no specific or concrete connotative value nor do they assist us in "visualizing" their antecedents. Their sole function is to "color" the mood of the work and to heighten the precious or decorative quality of the style. Typical are passages such as: "denn blaue Träume ziehn wie Spinnen/ um mich ein selig Wundernetz . . ." (SW III, 545: "because, like spiders, blue dreams/ draw around me a blessed, wonderous web . . ."); "Denn wir sind wie silberne Geigen/ in den Händen der Ewigkeit" (SW III, 636:

"For we are like silver violins/ in the hands of eternity"); "an Türen und an Herzen Pochen,/ flüchtiger Glanz in Silber und Kristall . . ." (SW III, 722: "on doors and on pulses, fleeting reflections in silver and crystal . . ."); "Sieben Gefühle aus Silber sind/ über deine dunkelspiegelnde Seele gespannt" (SW III, 623: "Seven emotions of silver are/ stretched across your darkly reflecting soul"). As indicated in these examples, Rilke preferred colors which evoke the decorative qualities of precious metals or jewels, particularly silver, and the pairing of the "emotions of the soul" with the color silver occurs especially frequently.

In much of his writing the poet also employed the devices of synesthesia and personification to intensify the atmosphere of a specific work and to direct attention to the way in which something occurs rather than what. The mixture of sense perception contributes measurably to the aura and the exquisite tone: ". . . kühle Becken,/ und mit den Händen ihre Lichte lecken/ und raten: Sind sie Silber oder Gold" (SW III, 227: ". . . cool basins/ and with my hands lick their lights/ and guess: Are they silver or gold"); ". . . und die Lampe singt zwischen ihnen merkwürdig laut" (SW IV, 245: ". . . and the lamp sings unusually loud between them"); "Ich soll silbern erzittern . . ." (SW I, 401: "I should tremble like silver . . ."). Furthermore, Rilke's tendency to endow certain inanimate objects with human characteristics also serves to underscore the rarified tone in his work. Objects are pensive, for example, or anxious, or tired; they tremble, and they get excited: "Am Pfad/ stehn alle Rosen in Gedanken . . ." (SW III, 238: "At the path/ all roses stand in thought . . ."); "Der Abend hob die Stirne aus dem Staube,/ die eines milden Wissens weise war" (SW III, 659: "The evening raised its countenance, which was wise from a mild wisdom, from the dust"); "Goldranken schlingen sich wie schlanke Tiere,/ die sich im Glanze ihrer Brünste gatten . . ." (SW I, 435: "Gold filigree entwines like slender beasts/ who mate in the splendor of their passion").

Rilke supported the emotionally charged mood of his works, moreover, by his particular use of similes. Though these phrases seem to serve the function of clarifying their "antecedents," they often possess only the vaguest relationship to them and in fact cannot be conceptualized in that context at all. They exist for their own sake and serve solely to underscore the particular tone of the poem. A typical example is a poem dedicated to Ludwig von Hofmann:

> Es legt sich dein Blick wie ein silberner Zügel
> um sie. Und lenkt sie in ruhigen Ronden.
> Und ihre Flügel,
> die selten schlagen,

sind wie Gefühle von Fraun,
von blonden.*   (SW III, 622)

The phrases "wie ein silberner Zügel" ("like a silver bridle"), and "wie Gefühle von Fraun,/ von blonden" ("like feelings of women,/ of blonds") have no intrinsic meaning for the poem nor do they assist us in visualizing or conceptualizing their antecedents, "dein Blick" ("your glance") and "ihre Flügel" ("her wings"). Their role is purely an emotional one: they contribute to the underlying mood. In another poem, the following appears:

> Nur die Mädchen fragen nicht,
> welche Brücke zu Bildern führe;
> lächeln nur, lichter als Perlenschnüre,
> die man an Schalen von Silber hält.†   (SW I, 374)

The relative clause, "die man an Schalen von Silber hält" ("that one holds against vessels of silver"), although apparently given the grammatical function of clarifying the antecedent "Perlenschnüre" ("strings of pearls"), actually attains an independence of its own. Its real purpose is to convey an expression of the "atmosphere of the soul." Many similar examples can be found throughout Rilke's works of the period, such as: "Nur dein Lächeln steht wie lauter Sterne/ über dir und bald auch über mir" (SW I, 485: "Only your smile stands like many stars/ above you and soon also over me"); "Zuseiten seines Streites/ stand, wie Türme stehen, ihr Gebet" (SW I, 618: "On the side of his struggle/ her prayer like towers stood"); and

> Nur einer Zeit zuliebe, die dich flehte
> in ihre klaren marmornen Gebete,
> erschienst du wie der König der Komete,
> auf deiner Stirne Strahlenströme stolz.‡   (SW I, 270)

The art of *Jugendstil* demonstrates, besides the emphasis on style and the underlying emotional tone, several other important features which Rilke adapted to his own writing as well. One of these was a concept concerning the composition of the work. Having freed himself from the apparent bondage of objective and "naturalistic" protrayal and

---

* "Your glance surrounds her like a silver bridle./ And guides her in subdued roundelays./ And her wings/ which rarely beat/ are like feelings of women,/ of blonds."

† "Only the maidens do not ask/ which bridges lead to pictures./ They smile only, lighter than strings of pearls/ that one holds against vessels of silver."

‡ "Only because of an era which begged it of you/ in its clear, marble prayers/ did you appear as the king of comets,/ on your forehead proudly streams of rays."

from the traditional strictures of perspective, symmetry, and the harmony of the "well-made" work, the Jugendstil artist, as we have seen,
could now compose his works in any form which he deemed advanta-
geous. Usually this form indicated a strong proclivity for the asymmetrical and the non-harmonious which exaggerated some elements in
the work, often the unexpected ones, while virtually ignoring others.
Through such compositional freedom, the artist was able to emphasize
whatever he thought appropriate and neglect that which he viewed as
insignificant. For this reason, many of these works were severely criticized at the time for having been poorly conceived and carried out, a
criticism reminiscent of that brought against Rodin to which Rilke so
forcefully spoke. A typical example of such asymmetrical composition
occurs in Gustav Klimt's "Danae." The figure of the woman has been
grossly exaggerated here in order to underscore certain of her features
which convey a particular emotion or tension. Thus the extreme curva-
ture of the neck, the broadened width of the thigh, the shortness of the
calf, and especially the twisted torso personify an increased primordial
strength, erotic tension, and voluptuousness. Such would not be the
case if the figure were portrayed more "realistically."

This compositional technique became an important element in
Rilke's writing as well. He too claimed the right to compose his works in
a purely subjective, "asymmetrical" form in which he could specifically
emphasize a particular feature and ignore others. From a traditional
point of view, his poems too might also have faced the charge of being
poorly conceived and haphazardly carried out, for they indeed demonstrate features contrary to a "well-made" appearance. In the poem
"Mondnacht," for example, the importance seems at first to lie with a
highly romanticized description of a moonlit landscape in southern
Germany. After a long stanza devoted to this description, however, the
emphasis is abruptly changed by the addition at the very end of the last
iambic line of a puzzling, mysterious, and entirely new element which
by its separation from the body of the poem and by its italicization
receives our full attention. In the process, the reader almost completely
forgets the long and involved description of the night. The poem in this
fashion assumes an "asymmetrical" form not unlike the works of Klimt
and other *Jugendstil* artists:

> Süddeutsche Nacht, ganz breit im reifen Monde,
> und mild wie aller Märchen Wiederkehr.
> Vom Turme fallen viele Stunden schwer
> in ihre Tiefen nieder wie ins Meer,—
> und dann ein Rauschen und ein Ruf der Ronde,

und eine Weile bleibt das Schweigen leer;
und eine Geige dann (Gott weiß woher)
erwacht und sagt ganz langsam:

Eine Blonde . . . *   (SW I, 372)

Approximately the same compositional emphasis occurs in "Du: / ein Schloß an wellenschweren."[6] In the poem, a castle in all its *Jugendstil* splendor and ornamentation recedes into the background as we ponder the implications of the word "jung" (young), although in this case, of course, the last element is not so foreign from the preceding context. Many similar forms occur in the poetry of the period.

In other works, it is the sheer amount of space devoted to any single element in the poem which may distinguish it and exaggerate its importance in relationship to any other. One such example is a poem written in 1898 which reminds us, by the way, of Peter Behrens's famous work "The Kiss":

Und dein Haar, das niederglitt,
nimm es doch dem fremden Winde,
an die nahe Birke binde
einen kußlang uns damit.†   (SW III, 602)

In the four lines of the first strophe, only three words indicate the presence of the lovers: "dein" (your), "nimm" (take), and "uns" (us). Our attention is directed rather to the hair itself, its blowing in the wind, and the birch tree to which it is to be bound. The more usual emphasis has thus been transferred to secondary elements of the poem which gain prominence by the number of lines they occupy. Many more such examples are to be found in Rilke's *Jugendstil* writing. One more example will suffice:

Das sind die Hände mit den schmalen
Gelenken, die sich leise mühn;
und wüßten die von Kathedralen,
sie müßten sich in Wundenmalen
vor allem Volke heiligblühn.‡   (SW I, 126)

* "South German night, all wide in the perfect moon,/ and mild like the return of all fairy tales./ From the tower, many hours fall heavily/ into its depths as into the sea.—/ And then a murmuring and a cry of the rounds,/ and for a time the silence remains empty;/ and a violin then (God knows from where)/ awakens and says very slowly:/ A Blond . . ."

† "And your hair that fell down/ take it from the foreign wind/ and bind on the birch nearby/ us with it for the length of a kiss."

‡ "Those are the hands with the small/ wrists that softly struggle;/ and if they knew about cathedrals,/ they would blossom forth/ with holy scars before all the people."

Again, the hands themselves are obscured by the plethora of details which fill the lines of this strophe. Much more important to the tone or aura of the poem are the small wrists, the cathedrals, and the holy scars in which the hands would blossom forth.

In addition to the ones discussed above, Rilke frequently adapted for his works two other basic elements of *Jugendstil*: the two-dimensional surface plane and the energized "whip-lash" line. In the visual arts of the period, as we have seen (cf. illus. 6), the artist composed his work in a series of closely related two-dimensional surface planes in order to eliminate the perception of foreground or background. He thus placed all the objects in his work at the same distance from the viewer, bestowing each with the same prominence. In this manner, the artist hoped to give his work a new unity and immediacy which he felt had been lost in the art of the recent past.

Rilke sought the same impression of unity and immediacy but utilized a stylistic device to produce it which was more traditional to his own medium of expression, namely that of temporal reference. By equating space with time and the lack of spatial depth with a lack of temporal sequence or orientation, the poet often created in his own works the same unified effect displayed by the visual arts. This he accomplished by various means, most of which are closely related to the verb and its insignificant role in the sentence. First of all, Rilke's works of the period display a lack of the more temporally restrictive tenses such as the present and past perfect and a marked preference for the present and the imperfect tenses which permit a much broader reference to time. The adverbs and adverbial phrases, so prominent in his sentences, are limited, in addition, primarily to the expression of manner and place, and modifiers of time appear remarkably seldom.

Certain passages in Rilke's works are particularly striking in their lack of temporal reference because of the paucity of finite verbs. In their place appear verbal nouns or infinitives which achieve the same astonishing effect of unity and simultaneity found in the typical *Jugendstil* work. In *Cornet Rilke*, the description of the festivities preceding the great battle includes the following:

Und war ein Wellenschlagen in den Sälen, ein Sich-vermischen und ein Sich-vermählen, ein Abschiednehmen und ein Wiederfinden, ein Glanzgenießen und ein Lichterblinden, ein Willigwerden jenen stillern Winden, die wie die Flügel fremder Blüten sind (SW III, 299).*

* "And there was a breaking of waves in the halls, a mixing of people and a uniting, a parting and finding each other again, an enjoyment of the brightness, a growing willingness for these quieter winds that are like the wings of strange blossoms."

All of the events seem to occur at the same time in a mixture of undifferentiated impressions, unified and immediate. In the poem "Intérieur," a series of sensual perceptions associated with the surroundings of a room are recorded with the same simultaneity by the substitution of infinitives in the sentences in place of subject and finite verb:

> So bleiben in den Wellen dieses Felles.
> Und wie zum Spiel durch müde Liderspalten
> den Formen folgen und den samtnen Falten,
> . . . .
>
> Und an den Vasen rütteln, daß ein Wellchen
> in ihnen aufwacht, und aus hellen Kelchen
> ein Blätterrieseln roter Rosen rollt.
>
> Und denken, denken: was das Klingen ist,
> und daß ein Duft ist wie von Mandarinen.
> Ob das die Seele von den Dingen ist
> und *über ihnen?* . . .*   (SW III, 227)

Coupled with this lack of finite verbs is the repeated occurance of the conjunction *und* which further weakens time differentiation and reinforces the unity of the passages. The poem "Die Konfirmanden" provides us with an additional example, combining as above, the use of verbal nouns and pharses and the unifying *und*:

> Das war ein Aufstehen zu dem weißen Kleide
> und dann durch Gassen ein geschmücktes Gehn
> und eine Kirche, innen kühl wie Seide,
> und lange Kerzen waren wie Alleen,
> und alle Lichter schienen wie Geschmeide,
> von feierlichen Augen angesehn.
>
> Und es war still, als der Gesang begann . . .†   (SW I, 387)

The final and most recognizable characteristic of *Jugendstil* to be considered here, the energized "whip-lash" line, also became an integral part of Rilke's works, not only as a motif where, as we have seen, it contributed to the more superficial aspects of the poet's involvement

---

* "Thus to remain in the waves of the fur./ And as in a game through tired eyelids/ to follow the forms and the velvet folds,/ . . ./ And to shake the vases so that a small wave/ awakens in them and from their lustrous necks/ rolls a rustling of leaves from red roses./ And to think, think: what that chiming is/ and that there is a fragrance as of mandarins./ Whether that is the soul of things/ and *above them*? . . ."

† "There was a getting up to white dresses/ and then a dressed-up walking through the streets/ and a church, inside cool as satin/ and long candles like pathways/ and all lights shone like jewels/ viewed by festive eyes./ And it was still when the singing began . . ."

6. *Gustav Klimt: "Portrait of Adele Bloch-Bauer"*
(Österreichische Galerie, Vienna)

with *Jugendstil*, but more importantly as one of his fundamental stylistic elements. To transform these undulating lines, Rilke often chose a wave-like variation of rhythm and tempo, alternations between elongated, sustained passages and pause, and the repetition of phrases. These devices convey the same energy and tension inherent in the "whiplash" lines of the visual arts and delineate as well one "surface plane" or element from another.

The poem "Die Stille," which, as we have seen, illustrates the *Wellen* motif, also incorporates many of the stylistic elements of the line:

> Hörst du, Geliebte, ich hebe die Hände—
> hörst du: es rauscht . . .
> Welche Gebärde der Einsamen fände
> sich nicht von vielen Dingen belauscht?
> Hörst du, Geliebte, ich schließe die Lider,
> und auch *das* ist Geräusch bis zu dir.
> Hörst du, Geliebte, ich hebe sie wieder . . .
> . . . aber warum bist du nicht hier.*   (SW I, 379)

This first stanza is endowed with the wave-like ebb and flow of energy and the tension of a *Jugendstil* work. This is achieved first of all by the fluctuation between the strong dactylic rhythm and the many irregularly prescribed pauses such as after "Hände" (hands), "rauscht" (murmurs), and "dir" (you). It is accomplished secondly by the juxtaposition of the extended statement, "Welche Gebärde der Einsamen fände / sich nicht von vielen Dingen belauscht?" ("which gesture of the solitary would not find / itself heard by many things?"), and the short, and in contrast, rather abrupt sentences, "hörst du, es rauscht" ("do you hear, it murmurs") and "aber warum bist du nicht hier" ("but why are you not here"). The repetition of the phrase "Hörst du" ("do you hear") heightens the wave-like effect. Furthermore, these repeated phrases serve to delineate, as it were, the various compositional units of the stanza with a bold outline.

In other works, it is the verse structure itself and the rhyme scheme which heighten the undulating effect in the poem. In such works, the tension builds slowly through a series of rhythmical pulsations until it reaches its apex, and also its release, at the very end of the stanza. The rhyme scheme supports this growing intensity and its release and defines as well the beginning and the termination of the energized "line." A passage from *Stunden-Buch* is typical:

---

* "Do you hear, lover, I raise my hands . . ./ do you hear, it murmurs . . ./ which gesture of the solitary would not find/ itself heard by many things?/ Do you hear, lover, I close my lids/ and *that* too is a sound reaching as far as you./ . . ./ . . . but why are you not here?"

Ich liebe dich, du sanftestes Gesetz,
an dem wir reiften, da wir mit ihm rangen;
du großes Heimweh, das wir nicht bezwangen,
du Wald, aus dem wir nie hinausgegangen,
du Lied, das wir mit jedem Schweigen sangen,
du dunkles Netz,
darin sich flüchtend die Gefühle fangen.*   (SW I, 268)

The first line, with its direct assertion, "Ich liebe dich, du sanftestes Gesetz" ("I love you, you softest of all laws"), and its masculine rhyme, marks the beginning of the *Jugendstil* "wave" and forms the foundation upon which the tension grows. In the second through fourth lines, this tension increases by means of the rhythmical pulsations, "du großes Heimweh . . ." ("you great feeling of homesickness . . ."), "du Wald . . ." ("you forest . . ."), and "du Lied . . ." (you song . . .") and by the same repeated feminine rhyme, "rangen," "bezwangen," "hinausgegangen," and "sangen." The fifth line represents both the climax of the tension as well as the beginning of its subsidence. The final repetition, "du dunkles Netz" ("you dark net"), the retardation of the tempo, and the prescribed pause at its end all emphasize the intensity of the line, while the masculine rhyme "Netz," which unites with "Gesetz" five lines earlier, signals the end of this "wave" and the commensurate release of tension, a process which is then rapidly completed by the final clause: "darin sich flüchtend die Gefühle fangen" ("in which fleeing all feelings are caught"). If several such stanzas follow one another in a poem, a situation akin to the series of parallel lines permeating the usual *Jugendstil* work is created.

The same or similar verse structure is evident on many occasions throughout Rilke's works of the period. For example, the following stanza appears in *Stunden-Buch*:

Denn du warst selber nur ein Gast des Golds.
Nur einer Zeit zuliebe, die dich flehte
in ihre klaren marmornen Gebete,
erschienst du wie der König der Komete,
auf deiner Stirne Strahlenströme stolz.†   (SW I, 270)

---

* "I love you, you softest of all laws/ from which we grew as we struggled with it./ You great feeling of homesickness, that we did not conquer,/ you forest from which we never went,/ you song that we sang with each silence,/ you dark net,/ in which fleeing all feelings are caught."

† "For you were yourself a guest of gold./ Only because of an era which begged it of you/ in its clear, marble prayers/ did you appear as the king of comets,/ on your forehead proudly streams of rays."

In *Buch der Bilder*, a comparable passage typifies Rilke's work at the height of his concern with *Jugendstil* structures:

> Mir lag im Haar der Ring.
> Und ich sprach ganz nahe und sachte,
> daß die Mutter nicht erwachte,—
> die an dasselbe dachte,
> wenn sie, ganz weiß gelassen,
> vor abendlichen Massen
> durch dunkle Gärten ging.*   (SW I, 426)

In each of these poems, the wave of tension begins in the first line, supported by the rhyme scheme and the structure, to build toward its apex and then finds its release and dissipates at the end of the strophe.

Through the investigation of stylistic features, it has become sufficiently evident—particularly when we add the evidence of Rilke's *Jugendstil* themes and the tenor of his critical writings—that the art and artists of *Jugendstil* exercised a fundamental influence on Rainer Maria Rilke during his vital formative years. By reinforcing certain of his natural proclivities toward style and certain of his innate feelings toward life, *Jugendstil* art assisted the poet in the realization of his artistic personality at a time when he was most susceptible to outside influences. As the relationship grew in intensity and as Rilke became more and more versed in the theories of this art, he was provided with the additional means of expressing his innermost thoughts and concerns. In the end, and by his own conscious attempt at adapting its most characteristic features, the influence of this art permeated his entire critical perception as well as the internal structure of all of his works. His decorative style, his alteration of syntactical structure, his asymmetrical composition, and his creation of literary "two-dimensional surface planes" and "undulating lines" provide us with the most obvious evidence. Later, like most of the artists of the movement, Rilke gradually abandoned, at least outwardly, many of the ideas of this period and became concerned with new forces in art and literature, for which to some extent *Jugendstil* art had provided the basis. Nevertheless, many of the qualities of this art echo throughout his later and more famous works. His relationship with *Jugendstil* had occurred at too crucial a period in his

---

* "In my hair lay the ring./ And I spoke very near and gently/ that mother would not awaken,—/ who thought of the same thing/ whenever she, entirely calm and white,/ before evening masses/ went through dark gardens."

early development to have been so quickly sublimated. It became a lasting force in his life, and it must be viewed as an integral part of an artistic personality which in subsequent years went on to produce some of the finest poetry of our century.

Notes

I. Introduction

[1] For Rilke's relationship with Cézanne and Rodin, consult K. A. J. Batterby, *Rilke and France: A Study in Poetic Development* (London, 1966), pp. 76–104. For his relationship to Paul Klee and Pablo Picasso see Herman Meyer, *Zarte Empirie* (Stuttgart, 1963), pp. 287–336.

[2] Bert Herzog, "Der Gott des Jugendstils in Rilkes Stundenbuch," *Schweizerische Rundchau*, 60/21 (1961), 1234–40.

[3] Ibid., p. 1238.

[4] Claude David, "Stefan George und der Jugendstil," *Formkräfte der deutschen Dichtung*, ed. H. Steffan (Göttingen, 1967), pp. 211–28.

[5] Paul Requadt, *Die Bildersprache der deutschen Italiendichtung von Goethe bis Benn* (Bern, 1962), pp. 172–86.

[6] Marieluise Champagne, "Rilke und der Jugendstil," Diss. Tulane, 1972.

[7] See Jost Hermand, *Jugendstil: Ein Forschungsbericht 1918–1964*. Referatheft der *Deutschen Vierteljahrsschrift* (1965).

[8] Fritz Schmalenbach, *Ein Beitrag zur Theorie und Geschichte der Flächenkunst* (Würzburg, 1935).

[9] Ernst Michalski, "Die entwicklungsgeschichtliche Bedeutung des Jugendstils," *Repertorium für Kunstwissenschaft*, 46 (1925), 133–49.

[10] Dolf Sternberger, "Jugendstil: Begriff und Physiognomie," *Die Neue Rundschau*, 45, II (1934), 255–71.

[11] Tschudi Madsen, *Art Nouveau* (New York, 1967).

[12] Hans Hofstätter, *Geschichte der europäischen Jugendstilmalerei* (Cologne, 1963).

[13] Wolfdietrich Rasch, "Fläche, Welle, Ornament: Zur Deutung der nachimpressionistischen Malerei und des Jugendstils," *Zur deutschen Literatur seit der Jahrhundertwende* (Stuttgart, 1967), 186–220.

[14] Elisabeth Klein, "Jugendstil in deutscher Lyrik," Diss. Cologne, 1957.

[15] Volker Klotz, "Jugendstil in der Lyrik," *Akzente*, 4 (1957), 26–34.

[16] Jost Hermand, *Lyrik des Jugendstils: Eine Anthologie mit einem Nachwort* (Stuttgart, 1964).

[17] Edelgard Hajek, *Literarischer Jugendstil* (Düsseldorf, 1971).

[18] Dominik Jost, *Literarischer Jugendstil* (Stuttgart, 1969).

[19] Jost Hermand, ed., *Jugendstil* (Darmstadt, 1971).

II. Rilke and Jugendstil

[1] Portions of this chapter appeared earlier in my article "Rainer Maria Rilke and the Art of Jugendstil," *The Centennial Review*, 15 (1972), 122–35.

[2] Rainer Maria Rilke, *Sämtliche Werke*, ed. Ernst Zinn (Frankfurt am Main, 1965), V, 329. Henceforth referred to as SW in the body of the text.

[3] All English translations in this study, unless otherwise designated, are my own and are designed to be as literal as possible.

[4] For example, Wolfdietrich Rasch, "Fläche, Welle, Ornament: Zur Deutung der nach-impressionistischen Malerei und des Jugendstils," *Zur deutschen Literatur seit der Jahrhundertwende* (Stuttgart, 1967), pp. 191–92.

[5] For a more detailed account of Rilke's acquaintance with other artists in Russia, particularly the Pasternaks, see André von Gronicka, "Rilke and the Pasternaks," *Germanic Review*, 27 (1952), 160–71. For an interesting account of Rilke's visit to the country estate of Tolstoy, see Eliza Maria Butler, *Rainer Maria Rilke* (Cambridge, 1941), pp. 55–56.

[6] Heinrich Vogeler, *Erinnerungen*, ed. Erich Weinert (Weimar, 1952), p. 75.

[7] R. M. Rilke, *Tagebücher aus der Frühzeit*, ed. Ruth Sieber-Rilke and Carl Sieber (Leipzig, 1942), 244–45.

[8] H. W. Petzet, *Von Worpswede nach Moskau: Heinrich Vogeler, Ein Künstler zwischen den Zeiten* (Cologne, 1972), p. 81.

[9] Ibid., p. 20.

[10] The exact details of this matter are recorded in a letter written in 1912 to Rilke's publisher. See Rilke, *Briefe an seinen Verleger*, ed. Ruth Sieber-Rilke and Carl Sieber (Leipzig, 1936), p. 147.

III. Rilke as an Art Critic

[1] Portions of this section appeared in my article "Rilke, Rodin, and Jugendstil," *Orbis Litterarum*, 27 (1972), 254–63.

[2] The monograph appeared in the Bard press in Berlin in 1903 with the title *Auguste Rodin*. It comprised 73 pages.

[3] Albert Elsen, *Rodin* (New York, 1963), p. 9.

[4] *The Connoisseur*, 119 (1947), 62–63.

[5] Although the subject of Rodin receives attention in most of the major works on Rilke, the most thorough analysis of the monograph has been written by Ursula Emde, *Rilke und Rodin* (Marburg/Lahn, 1949).

[6] Fritz Schmalenbach, *Ein Beitrag zur Theorie und Geschichte der Flächenkunst* (Würzburg, 1935), p. 36.

[7] Wolfdietrich Rasch, "Fläche, Welle, Ornament: Zur Deutung der nachimpressionistischen Malerei und des Jugendstils," *Zur deutschen Literatur seit der Jahrhundertwende* (Stuttgart, 1967), pp. 191–92.

[8] Tschudi Madsen, *Art Nouveau* (New York, 1967), p. 15.

[9] Rasch, p. 200.

IV. Jugendstil Themes in Rilke's Works

[1] Elisabeth Klein, "Jugendstil in deutscher Lyrik," Diss. Cologne, 1957, pp. 12–119.

[2] Edelgard Hajek, *Literarischer Jugendstil* (Düsseldorf, 1971), pp. 20–28, quotes several poems, for example, in which many "typical" motifs and themes appear without identifying them as to author or period. After allowing the reader the opportunity of assuming that these works belong to *Jugendstil*, she reveals that they are typical and rather well-known poems from the early 19th century.

[3] Klein, p. 87.

[4] Dolf Sternberger, *Über den Jugendstil und andere Essays* (Hamburg, 1956), pp. 16–17.

[5] Rainer Maria Rilke and Lou Andreas-Salomé, *Briefwechsel*, ed. Ernst Pfeiffer (Zurich, 1952), p. 19.

[6] Maurice Maeterlinck, *Le Trésor des Humbles* (Paris, 1931), p. 19.

[7] Horst Fritz, *Literarischer Jugendstil und Expressionismus: Zur Kunsttheorie, Dichtung und Wirkung Richard Dehmels* (Stuttgart, 1969), p. 92.

[8] For a thorough analysis of Rilke's religious orientation in *Stunden-Buch*, including a summary of the various critics' opinions about it, consult Eudo C. Mason's excellent chapter entitled "Zur Entstehung und Deutung von Rilkes Stunden-Buch" in his *Exzentrische Bahnen* (Göttingen, 1963), pp. 181–204.

[9] Dominik Jost, *Literarischer Jugendstil* (Stuttgart, 1969), p. 11.

[10] Hugo von Hofmannsthal, *Ausgewählte Werke*, ed. Rudolf Hirsch (Frankfurt am Main, 1957), p. 9.

[11] Rilke, *Tagebücher aus der Frühzeit*, pp. 153–54.

[12] Ibid., pp. 88–89.

[13] Paul Requadt, *Die Bildersprache der deutschen Italiendichtung von Goethe bis Benn* (Bern, 1962), pp. 173–74.

[14] Rilke, *Gesammelte Briefe*, ed. Ruth Sieber-Rilke and Carl Sieber (Leipzig, 1936–39), I, 332.

[15] For a complete analysis of the psychological implications of Rilke's "girlishness," of its origins and its effect on his work, consult Erich Simenauer, *Rainer Maria Rilke: Legende und Mythos* (Frankfurt am Main, 1953), pp. 231–309.

[16] Rilke, *Tagebücher aus der Frühzeit*, p. 257.

[17] Ibid., p. 284.

[18] Ibid., pp. 255–56.

V. Jugendstil Structure in Rilke's Works

[1] Compare pp. 74–75.

[2] Paul Requadt, *Die Bildersprache der deutschen Italiendichtung von Goethe bis Benn* (Bern, 1962), pp. 175 ff.

[3] Portions of this section appeared earlier in my article "Von Kunst zur Literatur: R. M. Rilkes literarischer Jugendstil," *Rilke heute: Beziehungen und Wirkungen*, ed. Ingeborg H. Solbrig and Joachim W. Storck (Frankfurt am Main, 1975), pp. 37–48.

[4] Dolf Sternberger, *Über den Jugendstil und andere Essays* (Hamburg, 1956), p. 15.

[5] H. W. Belmore, *Rilke's Craftsmanship* (Oxford, 1954), p. 17.

[6] Compare p. 52.

Chronology

1875: Born in Prague, 4 December.

1882: Attends the *Volksschule* in Prague.

1886: Enters the Military School at St. Pölten.

1890: Finishes school at St. Pölten (in June) and enters the Military School in Mährisch-Weißkirchen.

1891: Leaves the Military School in Mährisch-Weißkirchen (June) and attends the *Handelsakademie* (commercial school) in Linz.

1892: Return to Prague (May). Beginning of private study for *Abitur* (State Qualifying Examination).

1895: Successful completion of *Abitur* (July). Entrance to University for winter semester. *Larenopfer*.

1896: Move to Munich (end of September). *Traumgekrönt*.

1897: Stay in Munich (until beginning of October). 13 January, gives Liliencron lecture in Prague. March to middle of April, trip to Arco, Venice, Constance. June to August, stay in Wolfratshausen outside Munich. Move to Berlin-Wilmersdorf (beginning of October). *Advent*.

1898: Stay in Berlin (until end of July). March lecture about modern lyric in Prague. April and May, trip to Arco, Florence, Viareggio. Move to Berlin-Schmargendorf (31 July). Residence at Villa Waldfrieden (Andreas's villa). Middle to end of December, trip to Hamburg, Bremen, Worpswede. *Die weiße Fürstin* (First Version).

1899: Stay in Berlin-Schmargendorf. March, trip to Arco, Innsbruck, Prague, Vienna. 24 April, beginning of first trip to Russia. 27 April in Moscow; May in St. Petersburg; return 1 July. July to 12 September in Bibersberg bei Meiningen. *Mir zur Feier*, *Die Weise von Liebe und Tod des Cornets Christoph Rilke* (First Version), *Das Stunden-Buch* ("Das Buch vom mönchischen Leben").

1900: Stay in Berlin-Schmargendorf (until beginning of May). Beginning of May, second trip to Russia. 11 May in Moscow; 31 May to 5 July, Russian heartland; 5 July to 22 August, Moscow and St. Petersburg; 26 August return to Berlin. Stay in Worpswede with Heinrich Vogeler (27 August to 5 October). Stay in Berlin-Schmargendorf in own apartment in Misdroyer Straße 1. *Geschichten vom Lieben Gott*.

1901: Stay in Berlin-Schmargendorf (until end of February). March, trip to Munich, Arco, Riva, Bremen. Stay in Westerwede (beginning end of March after marriage to Clara Westhoff). *Das Stunden-Buch* ("Das Buch von der Pilgerschaft").

1902: Stay in Westerwede (until end of August). Middle of February the dedication of Bremer Kunsthalle. Move to Paris (arrives 27 August). 1 September, first meeting with Rodin. *Das Buch der Bilder* (First Version), *Worpswede*.

1903: Stay in Paris (until end of March). Stay in Viareggio (23 March–28 April). Stay in Paris (beginning 1 May). July and August, trip to Worpswede, Oberneuland. End of August, departure for Rome. Stay in Rome (beginning 10 September). *Auguste Rodin*.

1904: Stay in Rome (until end of June). Departure for Scandinavia in late June (Copenhagen, 24 June; Malmö, 25 June; Borgeby-gård, 26 June). Stay in Borgeby-gård with Ernst Norlind (26 June–19 August). Stay in Furuborg (September–December). *Die weiße Fürstin* (Final Version).

1905: Stay in Oberneuland (until end of February). Stay at Weißer Hirsch near Dresden (March until middle of April). Stay in Berlin (end of April–beginning of September). Move to Meudon-Val-Fleury outside Paris to serve as Rodin's secretary (15 September). 21 October–3 November, lecture trip to Cologne, Dresden, Prague, Leipzig. *Das Stunden-Buch* ("Das Buch von der Armut und vom Tode").

1906: Stay at Meudon (until 12 May). Move to Paris after breach with Rodin (12 May). 13 July–16 August, trip through Belgium. Move to Capri (4 December). *Das Buch der Bilder* (Final Version), *Die Weise von Liebe und Tod des Cornets Christoph Rilke* (Final Version).

1907: Stay in Capri (until 20 May). Move to Paris (31 May). Stay in Paris (throughout remainder of year). *Die Neuen Gedichte*.

Selected Bibliography

I have included here only books and articles related to this study. For a further and more complete bibliography of Rilke criticism, the reader is referred to:

Jonas, Klaus W. "Die Rilke-Kritik 1950–1966." *Insel-Almanach auf das Jahr 1967: Rainer Maria Rilke zum vierzigsten Todestag*. Frankfurt am Main, 1967. Pp. 94–121.
Ritzer, Walter. *Rainer Maria Rilke: Bibliographie*. Vienna, 1951.

Primary Works

Rilke, Rainer Maria. *Briefe an seinen Verleger*. Ed. Ruth Sieber-Rilke and Carl Sieber. Leipzig, 1936.
_____. *Gesammelte Briefe*. Ed. Ruth Sieber-Rilke and Carl Sieber. 6 vols. Leipzig, 1936–39.
_____. *Sämtliche Werke*. Ed. Ernst Zinn. 6 vols. Frankfurt am Main, 1955–1966.
_____. *Tagebücher aus der Frühzeit*. Ed. Ruth Sieber-Rilke and Carl Sieber. Leipzig, 1942.
_____ and Andreas-Salomé, Lou. *Briefwechsel*. Ed. Ernst Pfeiffer. Zurich, 1952.

Secondary Works

Ahlers-Hestermann, Friedrich. *Stilwende: Aufbruch der Jugend um 1900*. Berlin, 1941.
Andreas-Salomé, Lou. *Rainer Maria Rilke*. Leipzig, 1928.
Angelloz, Joseph A. *Rainer Maria Rilke: Leben und Werk*. Trans. Alfred Kuoni. Zurich, 1955.
Anon. Review of *Auguste Rodin* by R. M. Rilke. *The Connoisseur*, 119 (1947), 62–63.
Badt, Kurt. *Eine Wissenschaftslehre der Kunstgeschichte*. Cologne, 1971.
Baer, Lydia. "Rilke and Jens Peter Jacobsen." *PMLA*, 54 (1939), 900–32.

Barnstorff, Hermann. *"Pan, Jugend* und *Simplizissimus." Monatshefte,* 38 (1946), 284–92.

Batterby, K. A. J. *Rilke and France: A Study in Poetic Development.* London, 1966.

Behrens, Peter. *Feste des Lebens und der Kunst.* Jena, 1900.

Belmore, H. W. *Rilke's Craftsmanship.* Oxford, 1954.

Berendt, Hans. *Rainer Maria Rilkes Neue Gedichte: Versuch einer Deutung.* Bonn, 1957.

Blume, Bernhard. "Die Insel als Symbol in der deutschen Literatur." *Monatshefte,* 41 (1949), 239–47.

Böckmann, Paul. "Der Strukturwandel der modernen Lyrik in Rilkes Neuen Gedichten." *Wirkendes Wort,* 12 (1962), 336–54.

Bradley, Brigitte L. *R. M. Rilkes Neue Gedichte: Ihr zyklisches Gefüge.* Bern, 1967.

Brutzer, Sophie. *Rilkes russische Reisen.* Königsberg, 1934.

Butler, Eliza Maria. *Rainer Maria Rilke.* Cambridge, 1941.

Champagne, Marieluise. "Rilke und der Jugendstil." Diss. Tulane, 1972.

Clements, Robert J. "Rilke, Michelangelo and the *Geschichten vom lieben Gott." Studies in Germanic Languages and Literature: Festschrift for Ernst A. G. Rose.* Ed. Robert A. Fowkes and Volkmar Sander. Reutlingen, 1967. Pp. 57–70.

Corcoran, Mary B. "Zur Bedeutung wichtiger Wörter in den frühen Schriften von Rilke." Diss. Bryn Mawr, 1958.

Curjel, Hans. "Vom neunzehnten zum zwanzigsten Jahrhundert." *Ausstellungskatalog der Ausstellung "Um 1900" des Kunstgewerbemuseums Zürich.* Zurich, 1952. Pp. 7–20.

David, Claude. "Stefan George und der Jugendstil." *Formkräfte der deutschen Dichtung.* Ed. Hans Steffen. Göttingen, 1963. Pp. 211–28.

Demetz, Peter. *René Rilkes Prager Jahre.* Düsseldorf, 1953.

Edfelt, Britz. "Rilke ock konstnärerna i Worpswede." *Studiekamraten,* 48 (1965), 30–33.

Egenhoff, Manfred. "Zur Textgrundlage der biblischen Gedichte in Rainer Maria Rilkes *Neuen Gedichten." Wirkendes Wort,* 18 (1969), 245–49.

Elsen, Albert. *Rodin.* New York, 1963.

Emde, Ursula. *Rilke und Rodin.* Marburg/Lahn, 1949.

Fechter, Paul. "Nietzsches Bildwelt und der Jugendstil." *Deutsche Rundschau,* 243 (1935), 30–36.

Forster, Leonard. "An unpublished Letter from Rilke to Kokoschka." *German Life and Letters,* 15 (1961–62), 21–24.

Fritz, Horst. *Literarischer Jugendstil und Expressionismus: Zur Kunsttheorie, Dichtung und Wirkung Richard Dehmels.* Stuttgart, 1969.

Goertz, Hartmann. *Frankreich und das Erlebnis der Form im Werke Rainer Rilkes.* Stuttgart, 1932.

Gronicka, André von. "Rilke and the Pasternaks." *Germanic Review*, 27 (1952), 260–71.

Hajek, Edelgard. *Literarischer Jugendstil*. Düsseldorf, 1971.

Hamann, Richard and Hermand, Jost. *Stilkunst um 1900*. Berlin, 1967.

Hell, Victor. "Tradition und Ursprünglichkeit in Rilkes Werken: Über die Beziehungen zwischen Dichtung und Malerei." *Tradition und Ursprünglichkeit*. Akten des III. Internationalen Germanistenkongresses in Amsterdam, 1965. Pp. 189–90.

Hermand, Jost. "Gesang der Frauen an den Dichter." *Monatshefte*, 56 (1964), 49–60.

———, ed. *Jugendstil*. Darmstadt, 1971.

———. *Jugendstil: Ein Forschungsbericht 1918–1964*. Referatheft der *Deutschen Vierteljahrsschrift*, 1965.

———. *Lyrik des Jugendstils: Eine Anthologie mit einem Nachwort*. Stuttgart, 1964.

———. "Undinen-Zauber: Zum Frauenbild des Jugendstils." *Wissenschaft als Dialog*. Ed. Renate von Heydebrand and Klaus Günther Just. Stuttgart, 1969. Pp. 9–29.

Herzog, Bert. "Der Gott des Jugendstils in Rilkes Stundenbuch." *Schweizerische Rundschau*, 60/21 (1961), 1237–41.

Hocke, Gustav René. *Die Welt als Labyrinth: Manier und Manie in der europäischen Kunst*. Hamburg, 1957.

Hofmannsthal, Hugo von. *Ausgewählte Werke*. Ed. Rudolf Hirsch. Frankfurt am Main, 1957.

Hofstätter, Hans. *Geschichte der europäischen Jugendstilmalerei*. Cologne, 1963.

Houston, Gertrude Craig. "Rilke's *Buch der Bilder*." *Modern Language Review*, 29 (1934), 333–36.

Howarth, Thomas. *Charles Rennie Mackintosh and the Modern Movement*. London, 1952.

Hunt, John Dixon. *The Pre-Raphaelite Imagination: 1848–1900*. Lincoln, Nebraska, 1968.

Jost, Dominik. "Jugendstil und Expressionismus." *Expressionismus als Literatur*. Ed. Wolfgang Rothe. Bern, 1969. Pp. 87–106.

———. *Literarischer Jugendstil*. Stuttgart, 1969.

Klein, Elisabeth. "Jugendstil in deutscher Lyrik." Diss. Cologne, 1957.

Klotz, Volker. "Jugendstil in der Lyrik." *Akzente*, 4 (1957), 26–34.

Langenheim, Karin. "Das Buch der Bilder: Entstehung und Deutung." Diss. Kiel, 1962.

Lehnert, Herbert. "Satirische Botschaft an den Leser: Das Ende des Jugendstils." *Gestaltungsgeschichte und Gesellschaftsgeschichte*. Ed. Helmut Kreuzer. Stuttgart, 1969. Pp. 487–515.

Lenning, Walter. "Der literarische Jugendstil." *Deutsche Universitäts-Zeitung*, 13 (1958), 423–28.

Madsen, Tschudi. *Art Nouveau*. New York, 1967.

Maeterlinck, Maurice. *Le Trésor des Humbles*. Paris, 1913.

Mason, Eudo C. *Exzentrische Bahnen*. Göttingen, 1963.

Meyer, Herman. *Zarte Empirie*. Stuttgart, 1963.

Michalski, Ernst. "Die entwicklungsgeschichtliche Bedeutung des Jugendstils." *Repertorium für Kunstwissenschaft*, 46 (1925), 133–49.

Mises, Richard von, ed. *Rainer Maria Rilke: Bücher, Theater, Kunst*. Vienna, 1934.

_____. *R. M. Rilke im Jahre 1896*. 3 vols. New York, 1944–46.

Mövius, Ruth. *Rainer Maria Rilkes Stundenbuch: Entstehung und Gehalt*. Leipzig, 1937.

Mühlher, Robert. "Rilke und Cézanne: Eine Studie über die künstlerische Methode." *Österreich in Geschichte und Literatur*, 10 (1966), 35–47.

Obrist, Hermann. *Neue Möglichkeiten in der bildenden Kunst (1896–1900)*. Jena, 1903.

Petzet, H. W. *Von Worpswede nach Moskau: Heinrich Vogeler, Ein Künstler zwischen den Zeiten*. Cologne, 1972.

Rasch, Wolfdietrich. *Zur deutschen Literatur seit der Jahrhundertwende*. Stuttgart, 1967.

Requadt, Paul. *Die Bildersprache der deutschen Italiendichtung von Goethe bis Benn*. Bern, 1962.

_____. "Jugendstil im Frühwerk Thomas Manns." *Deutsche Vierteljahrsschrift*, 40 (1966), 206–16.

Rolleston, James. *Rilke in Transition*. New Haven, 1970.

Salzmann, Karl H. "Pan: Geschichte einer Zeitschrift." *Archiv für Geschichte des Buchwesens*, 1 (1958), 212–25.

Schmalenbach, Fritz. *Ein Beitrag zur Theorie und Geschichte der Flächenkunst*. Würzburg, 1935.

_____. "Jugendstil und Neue Sachlichkeit." *Das Werk*, 24 (1937), 129–34.

Schmutzler, Robert. *Art Nouveau—Jugendstil*. Stuttgart, 1962.

Selig, Helmut, ed. *Jugendstil: Der Weg ins 20. Jahrhundert*. Heidelberg/Munich, 1959.

Simenauer, Erich. *Rainer Maria Rilke: Legende und Mythos*. Frankfurt am Main, 1953.

Sternberger, Dolf. "Jugendstil: Begriff und Physiognomie." *Die neue Rundschau*, 45/II (1934), 255–71.

_____. *Über den Jugendstil und andere Essays*. Hamburg, 1956.

Sterner, Gabriele. *Jugendstil: Kunstformen zwischen Individualismus und Massengesellschaft*. Cologne, 1975.

Tubach, Frederick. "The Image of the Hand in Rilke's Poetry." *PMLA*, 76 (1961), 240–46.

Uhlig, Helmut. "Vom Ästhetizismus zum Expressionismus." *Expressionismus*. Ed. Hermann Friedmann and Otto Mann. Heidelberg, 1956.

Van de Velde, Henry. *Geschichte meines Lebens*. Ed. Hans Curjel. Munich, 1962.

Vogeler, Heinrich. *Erinnerungen*. Ed. Erich Weinert. Weimar, 1952.

Webb, Karl E. "Rainer Maria Rilke and the Art of Jugendstil." *The Centennial Review*, 15 (1972), 122–35.

———. "Rilke, Rodin, and Jugendstil: The Poet as an Art Critic." *Orbis Litterarum*, 27 (1972), 254–63.

———. "Von Kunst zur Literatur: R. M. Rilkes literarischer Jugendstil." *Rilke heute: Beziehungen und Wirkungen*. Ed. Ingeborg H. Solbrig and Joachim W. Storck. Frankfurt am Main, 1975. Pp. 37–48.

Wegels, Herbert. "Heinrich Vogeler und der Jugendstil." Diss. Göttingen, 1959.

Wocke, Helmut. *Rilke und Italien*. Gießener Beiträge zur deutschen Philologie, vol. 73. Gießen, 1940.

Name and Title Index

UNIVERSITY OF NORTH CAROLINA
STUDIES IN THE GERMANIC LANGUAGES
AND LITERATURES

For other volumes in the "Studies" see page ii and following page.

Send orders to: (U.S. and Canada)
The University of North Carolina Press, P.O. Box 2288
Chapel Hill, N.C. 27514
(All other countries) Feffer and Simons, Inc., 31 Union Square, New York, N.Y. 10003

UNIVERSITY OF NORTH CAROLINA
STUDIES IN THE GERMANIC LANGUAGES
AND LITERATURES

71. Murray A. and Marian L. Cowie, eds. THE WORKS OF PETER SCHOTT (1460–1490). Volume II: Commentary. Pp. xxix, 534. Paper $13.00. (See also volume 41.)
72. Christine Oertel Sjögren. THE MARBLE STATUE AS IDEA: COLLECTED ESSAYS ON ADALBERT STIFTER'S *DER NACHSOMMER*. 1972. Pp. xiv, 121. Cloth $7.00.
73. Donald G. Daviau and Jorun B. Johns, eds. THE CORRESPONDENCE OF ARTHUR SCHNITZLER AND RAOUL AUERNHEIMER WITH RAOUL AUERNHEIMER'S APHORISMS. 1972. Pp. xii, 161. Cloth $7.50.
74. A. Margaret Arent Madelung. THE LAXDOELA SAGA: ITS STRUCTURAL PATTERNS. 1972. Pp. xiv, 261. Cloth $9.25.
75. Jeffrey L. Sammons. SIX ESSAYS ON THE YOUNG GERMAN NOVEL. 1972. Pp. xiv, 187. Cloth $7.75.
76. Donald H. Crosby and George C. Schoolfield, eds. STUDIES IN THE GERMAN DRAMA. A *FESTSCHRIFT* IN HONOR OF WALTER SILZ. 1974. Pp. xxvi, 255. Cloth $10.75.
77. J. W. Thomas. TANNHÄUSER: POET AND LEGEND. With Texts and Translations of his Works. 1974. Pp. x, 202. Cloth $10.75.
78. Olga Marx and Ernst Morwitz, trans. THE WORKS OF STEFAN GEORGE. 1974. 2nd, rev. and enl. ed. Pp. xxviii, 431. Cloth. $12.90.

For other volumes in the "Studies" see preceding page and p. ii.

For other volumes in the "Studies" see preceding page and p. ii.

Send orders to: (U.S. and Canada)
The University of North Carolina Press, P. O. Box 2288
Chapel Hill, N.C. 27514
(All other countries) Feffer and Simons, Inc., 31 Union Square, New York, N.Y. 10003

Volumes 1–44 and 46–49 of the "Studies" have been reprinted.
They may be ordered from:
AMS Press, Inc., 56 E. 13th Street, New York, N.Y. 10003
For a complete list of reprinted titles write to:
Editor, UNCSGL&L, 442 Dey Hall, 014A, UNC, Chapel Hill, N.C. 27514